Lives

&

Tales from Two Cities

edited by Jane Bernstein
& Rodge Glass

CARGO
publishing

"Second Lives: Tales From Two Cities"
Edited by Jane Bernstein & Rodge Glass
First Published 2012
Published by Cargo Publishing
SC376700
978-1-908885-02-9
Bic Code-JF Society and culture: general
FYB Short Stories

Produced with assistance from:
Creative Scotland
The University of Strathclyde
Carnegie Mellon University

Also available as:
Ebook
Kindle ebook
Enhanced ebook
App for iPad

Printed & Bound in England by CPI

Cover design by Sarah-Louise McKay & Craig Lamont
Typeset by Craig Lamont

www.cargopublishing.com

This book is dedicated to the citizens of
Glasgow & Pittsburgh

Contents

Introduction
Jane Bernstein & Rodge Glass

Jane Bernstein: Let's start with you. When did you first arrive in Glasgow?

Rodge Glass: Well, the first time I entered Glasgow I was on my way to live there. It was 1997, I was driving north from Manchester in my Grandma's old Nissan Starlet, and I'd insisted I didn't want help from my family. I was nineteen, after all. And I'd just come back from a year in Israel, most recently Kibbutz Yahel, where I'd worked picking Pomelos in the shadow of the Jordanian mountains, making friends from all over the world and working out I wasn't a Zionist. Compared to that, surely this was no big deal. Okay, I was only coming to Glasgow because I'd failed my exams and been turned down by my first choice University. I'd never been to Scotland. Everything I thought I knew had been learned from Irvine Welsh's novel Trainspotting - and that was set in Edinburgh. CHOOSE LIFE said the Trainspotting poster on my wall, and that's what I planned to do. After all, people are just people, right? A place is like any other place. The first I saw of Glasgow was the sign visible from the motorway reading 'Glasgow's Miles Better', alongside a big yellow Mr Happy face.

I only learned later that this was part of a mid-1980's campaign designed to kick-start a change of Glasgow's negative image as a place of poverty, violence and not much else besides. That change has been underway since then, propelled by Glasgow being chosen as the European City of Culture in 1990, a title which brought a great deal of attention, outside money, and renovation too. This was controversial with some of the city's artistic community - but others felt the title went a long way to helping Glasgow get rid of the reputation for being grim, dark, dangerous. I don't think that was ever true of the place, but as the traditional industries died, it needed to find a new way to breathe and 21st Century Glasgow is now far more international, multi-cultural, outward-looking. Not that I appreciated any of this on my arrival. In 1997, I lasted three months in University halls at Strathclyde. I was ignored by my stoner flatmates. I was too impatient and immature to study. I couldn't find anywhere I liked being. So I switched classes, joined a band and moved to the East End, in a tiny flat next to the Tennent's brewery and opposite the abattoir, and from there I started again. That was probably my lowest point in the city. I didn't know what I was doing here. I couldn't imagine how I could stay. But then I started playing gigs, going to a writing group, and realised that there was a huge subculture in Glasgow that was rich, and welcoming, and couldn't care less what was considered fashionable elsewhere. Which was incredibly freeing. 15 years later that community of people who make imagined things and support others that do the same is the very centre of my life here. It has shaped me more than any other place, it has nothing whatsoever to do with money, and I would have been lost without it. So. It seems we're already into therapy here, Jane! That didn't take long. You're from New York – the centre of the universe. How the hell did you end up in Pittsburgh?

JB: The beginning of the long road that lead me to Pittsburgh was the Fillmore East, Bill Graham's old rock palace on Second Avenue and 6th Street in New York, where I worked from 1968 – 1971. The manager of the Fillmore, and several members of the stage crew, who did lighting, sound design, the light show, were brilliant and innovative and had gone to this university I knew nothing about called Carnegie Tech, in this city I'd never visited with the most unappealing name. Pittsburgh. In 1991, twenty years after the Fillmore closed, I decided it was time to look for a full-time teaching job, which meant leaving the NY metro area, where I had lived my entire life. And, yes, it was a really wrenching decision. If I was going to move, I was determined to live somewhere interesting and be at a high-energy university, so when I saw this opening at Carnegie Mellon, I remembered the stage crew at the Fillmore and thought if I had to leave the center of the universe, this might not be such a bad place. During the second step of the hiring process, I met Hilary Masters and Sharon Dilworth, and I thought: this is good, then I read Cooper, a novel of Hilary's, and "This Month of Charity," a short story of Sharon's and I thought, this is very good. Then I visited the city and went down to Penn Mac in the Strip and I saw the big barrels of olives, and I thought: okay, I can live here.

I had a husband and two kids and bought a big brick house on Beechwood Blvd. in Squirrel Hill — the same street where Jerry Stern had lived as a child — and wondered when I'd say "Squirrel Hill" without laughing. My neighbors on either side – all four of them MDs – brought over wine, bread, and cheese, and when the moving van arrived, a Thermos of coffee and cups, welcoming us in a way I had never experienced anywhere else. I started to make my way around campus, learning where the women's rooms were and trying to be less anxious about not having read Derrida. Because I am seriously directionally challenged, navigating Pittsburgh, with its rivers and hills and bridges -- 446 of them -- was beyond my ability, so for about a year, I stayed in the neighborhoods nearest the university. One day, my neighbor's father, a government professor at Cornell University who'd grown up in Pittsburgh, asked me what I thought about the city. It was summer and the lawns were green and the all along the leafy boulevard all the gardens were in bloom, and I said that it was a nice place, that like others who'd grown up elsewhere and thought of Pittsburgh as grim and gritty, I'd been surprised how clean the city was now that the blast furnaces were gone. It felt kind of like a college town, I said, because nearly everyone I knew was at a university or the huge medical center. My airy response displeased him. You have no idea how devastated the city was by the loss of industry, he said. Then he set about to tell me.

His words shamed me and piqued my interest in learning about the city's history and became a first lit point in my zigzagging journey to get to know Pittsburgh. A short time after that, I went to a plumbing supply store in Braddock. I'd known that Andrew Carnegie's Edgar

Thompson Steel Works had been in Braddock, that it was the site of the first Carnegie Library, and that the city had been decimated after the mill closed. The buildings on the main street gave evidence that it had been a vibrant place, but it had been emptied out -- ninety percent of its population was gone. Driving past the boarded-up buildings, seeing what had become of Braddock, was a second point in beginning to grasp the past and present of this city that had become my home. The third point occurred in 1995, when the Associated Writing Program had its annual meeting in Pittsburgh, and poets Jack Gilbert and Gerald Stern, native sons, gave readings. By then, I knew more of the city's history, but when I thought of the city's industrial past, I still thought of it as a miserable place, smoky and polluted, where men changed their shirts twice a day. These two poets brought images of the city of their childhood as a muscular city, where those blast furnaces lit up the sky and men made steel for bridges and ships, and the bars that lined the streets of the city and surrounding towns were packed. "Sumptuous-shouldered," in Gilbert's "Searching for Pittsburgh:" "Sleek-thighed, obstinate and majestic…" ""Beautiful filthy Pittsburgh," in Stern's "The Dancing." I listened and for the first time truly began to understand the depth of what the region had lost.

The fourth point in my journey began when I got a GPS and no longer feared that if I got lost I'd never find my way back home. I began to venture further. Thanks to Pittsburgh's constant road construction (the joke is that Pennsylvania's state flower is the construction cone), I often find myself completely turned around, in an area of the city I never knew existed, an old enclave that feels lost in time, dominated by a grand church, houses packed together on steep streets, Steelers flags hung in the windows, only now instead of being fearful that I'd be stranded forever, I find these wrong turns interesting, sometimes exhilarating.

Working on this book has been the fifth point – thanks to our contributors, I've seen the city from so many new vantage points... But I've gone on long enough, so I'll turn to you. When did you start to feel as if you knew Glasgow? Or don't you?

RG: Until I develop a Glaswegian accent – which, at my age, is pretty unlikely now – I don't think I'll ever feel like I know the city in the same way someone born here would do. I feel close to people and places, I even feel there's something in the personality of the city that's held me here all these years – Glasgow keeps me warm but keeps me grounded, and I even believe Glasgow is with me somehow, wherever I go. Still, as long as I open my mouth and an English voice comes out, especially in these times when independence is such a hot topic, I think I'll always be aware that the city isn't mine. I'm sure that's a pretty regular immigrant's experience; the fact that taxi drivers sometimes think I'm here on holiday (and ask when I'm going home) has never got in the way of my becoming part of this city. And not once in fifteen years has anyone in the artistic community made me feel like I don't belong here – on the contrary, I've been invited all over the world to represent Scotland, and I'm proud to do it. Sometimes I have a bit of a laugh about how the Scots are a little like the Jews. Once they feel you're one of them, there's no getting away: it's a life sentence. I think I'll always be talked about as a Scottish writer now. And even my most English books will be on the shelf in bookshops under the title 'Scottish Fiction'.

For me, knowing the city and being a writer in the city has always been part of the same thing. Because it was the writing community that gave me something to belong to, a social life, and friends. When I moved here I'd never been to a reading, a book launch, a festival, nothing. I had never taken a serious interest in the work of a living writer and certainly didn't think this was something you could choose to do with your life. Glasgow has a hugely vibrant literary world, and seeing how it worked made me want to contribute to it. That's partly the reason why I wanted to edit the The Year of Open Doors anthology. I felt I was one of many writers who had come to Scotland and, for one reason or another, decided to make a life here. That was simply not happening 30 years ago. (Edwin Morgan described the publishing scene in Scotland in the 1970s as being like 'a wasteland'.) I felt Scotland (and more specifically, Glasgow, as that's my home) was now an open minded, internationally-flavoured place which was becoming confident enough to welcome in others like me. So I included adopted Scots from South Africa, Zimbabwe, Bulgaria and Canada in that book, along with local young voices who deserved a platform. It was a statement of intent, also of how the city was changing.

I don't think there's ever been a point where I was certain of feeling like I knew Glasgow, but I do remember being first truly excited by it. I was in the 13th Note Café in 1998, there for about my second or third gig that week. The gigs there, then and now, take place in a dingy, dark underground room with virtually no decoration where the band plays on the same level as the audience and the sound is pretty basic. I went to see a band everyone seemed to know about but I'd never heard of. They were called El Hombre Trajeado. Apparently they'd been played by the legendary uncoverer of talent, DJ John Peel on his late night show. Back then, lots of people who hung out in the 13th Note wore their T-Shirts – until now I thought El Hombre Trajeado was a brand name. Anyway, the room was so packed for this gig on a Tuesday night that you couldn't move, so even though I could see virtually nothing, there was no point even trying to get a better view. The best you could hope for was to sway a little, following the beat. Most songs were instrumentals and the guitar player lurched back and forward, lost, looking at the ground. There was a DJ in the band, playing what appeared to be old (probably out-of-copyright) sounds from the BBC archive underneath it, with a tight, intricate rhythm section who moved to the dropped beats, jumped around and couldn't stop grinning. Everyone in the audience seemed to know all these songs, but how? It was so hot in there, I was dripping sweat. I remember looking across at my friend Paul and laughing. 'Welcome to Glasgow!' he said. By which he meant: We do not care at all what's going on out there in the world. We know this doesn't make sense to people from outside and we don't need permission from them. I found that incredibly empowering, and I've been interested in that independent, ground-up spirit ever since, which has always seemed strong here.

And it has always remained intimate. Glasgow's population is big enough to be diverse, but small enough for me to keep bumping into the same people over the years, in different guises. I saw that band many times more in that venue, and many times elsewhere. It was a Glasgow night out, and they were never once a let down. The musicians have all gone on to do interesting things, too. I saw the guitarist, Hubby, who's now playing a beautiful kind of Glasgow-flamenco guitar under the name RM Hubbert, last month in The Arches, a venue which runs directly under Central Station – the floor rumbles when trains pass overhead. Many of the faces in the audience were the same as back in 98 – only now we were sitting at tables. Hubby has recorded an album with his favourite Scottish musicians, and so was inviting this or that one to join him for a song. One of whom was in El Hombre, and others were in the bands I fell in love with when I first moved here. Arab Strap. The Delgados. The bands that, via the lyrics of their songs, the streets and pubs referenced, the language and the wit, helped me find a way into the city. It was a quiet night at The Arches. I only had two beers. But my old friend Paul came with me, and I remember thinking this was probably as close as I was ever going to get to feeling like I knew Glasgow, in this place of people who make imagined things. And that it was my home.

JB: Your mentor and friend Alasdair Gray describes himself as a "maker of imagined things." It's an expression I know you like yourself. Let's talk about this imagined thing we call Second Lives and how it came to be.

RG: It came about through the exchange programme between my university and yours. In Spring 2010 I visited Pittsburgh on behalf of Strathclyde University – I went to meet academics over there and try to learn something from the way Carnegie Mellon University was running its undergraduate program. I also went to give a reading from my own work and explore the city. During my stay I became interested not only in Pittsburgh itself, but also in the remarkable collection of writers working at CMU. I read Jane McCafferty's One Heart, Sharon Dilworth's The Long White and Terrance Hayes' Hip Logic. Before I landed back in Scotland I was plotting a collaboration.

JB: Then I visited Glasgow in the fall of 2010, when you were my host. It was a whirlwind couple of days – a presentation at Strathclyde, drinks that night at Babbity Bowster with the Strathclyde writers, a celebration at the Oran Mor for Alasdair Gray, which included a reading by Louise Welsh, more drinks, more great conversation, then back to the Babbity Bowster, and up a set of narrow steps to my lodgings for this visit. When I came home, I couldn't stop talking about this amazing city, with its godawful weather, even worse than Pittsburgh's, and an incredibly vibrant cultural life, everywhere I went people making music and writing stories and poems and plays. It seemed to be spilling out of people, in a way that felt joyful, whereas so many of the conversations I'd been having with writer friends at home were about sales figures and corporate publishing and the death of the traditional book. I also reported to my friends in Pittsburgh that in Glasgow no one eats dinner.

RG: Yeah, sorry about that. I get overexcited sometimes. And forget to feed guests....

JB: To me, it was yet another sign that you writers in Glasgow were on another plane entirely, while I, mere earthbound mortal, after my second night without solid food, had a very late dinner before I climbed upstairs to bed. (Mornings, I had porridge in the pub, a real treat.) Of course I knew I was being the kind of tourist who makes loud, confident pronouncements while knowing almost nothing, but I didn't care. I had a big giant crush on Glasgow.

The other important part of this trip was meeting Mark Buckland and hearing about Cargo Publishing. Forget that he was practically a child -- I liked the way he talked about books and I liked the way he produced and distributed them. This was definitely part of my big crush.

RG: Ha! Mark will read that and think you have a big crush on him. (Which I kind of do too.) He says being boss of Cargo is like being President of the United States – a four-year term ages you two decades. Anyway – don't let me get distracted. Maybe we should explain how the book came about?

JB: The first thought for me was simply that there were so many talented writers at Strathclyde and CMU, doing such a range of really fine work – enough good writing to fill a book! And, of course, there were our cities, Glasgow and Pittsburgh, and all they had in common. Both are cities that lost their major traditional industries and had to reinvent themselves for the 21st century; both struggled, lost population, grappled with urban woes, and reinvigorated; both are full of rich culture, not always acknowledged outside their borders. When we started to contact writers at our universities, we asked if they were interested in submitting a "creative response" to post-industrial Pittsburgh or Glasgow. We wanted new work. Beyond that, we had no parameters. As the project became broader and more ambitious, I began to see that the larger goal of our project – to show our cities to readers – was also a way of showing our cities to each other.

When I sent you Lori Jakiela's "Psychic Spiritual Advisor to the Stars," it took some effort not to include a little postscript saying: this is what life is like in Pittsburgh. (The psychic is in Butler, not Pittsburgh, but even so...). This is also what life is like! I wanted to shout, after I read Hilary Masters' lovely evocation of an evening at the ballpark, "One Spring Afternoon." I felt like a tour guide, trying to take you on one of those off-the-beaten-track tours of a city, meant to show the visitor something beyond the usual loop of monuments and museums. Reading the selections from Glasgow has deepened my desire not merely to return but to stay for a while. I'll never meet the boy who wanders through the partially-built houses of a subdivision in Allan Wilson's powerful story, "Remember When This Was a Farm?," or the Tesco cashier in Ewan Morrison's

"Where, Who and Why," but these characters give me a sense of what life is like in different corners of your city.

Obviously, no single story or poem can capture a diverse, ever-changing city. It takes a collection for a sense of a place to emerge, many stories, and many images. After the submissions arrived from the writers, we looked to visual artists, and they provided extraordinary photography, drawings and 'dialectograms' – Mitch Mitchell's invented word for his intricate drawings. Although we always intended for an ebook to be released along with the traditional book, once we turned to the visual artists, plans for an enhanced version were made, so ebook readers will also be able to see short films by Doug Cooper, and Peter Mackie Burns along with extensive multimedia content we hope adds a meaningful extra dimension. Together, all these forms give the reader a deeper appreciation of the familiar and access into the unknown. Don't you think?

RG: The longer this process has gone on, the more I've become fond of the idea of exploring Pittsburgh via my New York Tour Guide, sending me this or that taste of Pittsburgh via my email inbox. As you told me, in order to get to know the place a little, you need to spend time in the neighbourhoods, each of which has its own character and history. Perhaps part of that can be done in the imagination. I hope that, like me, readers who don't know Pittsburgh can open this book, climb into these tales and start that process. Sit at the bar in Tessaro's in Bloomfield, with its pressed tin ceilings, and wait for Ruth to bring them a beer. Maybe later that night, meet Wanda C., with her tattooed forearms. Walk down a side street in Squirrel Hill, past the grand houses until you find Maggie's tent up in Sam's backyard. As for me, I want to look out for Lee at Starbucks in Shadyside at six AM. More than anything, I want to follow Charlee's West Highland Terrier around the basketball courts and under the bridges of Pitt, seeing and sniffing what's so interesting from down there, close to the ground. Writer, fictional character, dog, it's all the same – each of them can show me something of the life of the city. Similarly, I hope readers on your side of the Atlantic will see the Clyde river as Louise does, take a night walk with Will, contrast David Kinloch's Glasgow to Edwin Morgan's, see its streets through Gordon's photographs and its symbols through Richard Wilson's history of the Old Firm. And maybe afterwards they'll want to keep looking. In one of these stories, Doug Johnstone's, they may even recognise Babbity Bowster, where you treated yourself to breakfast. Perhaps that particular scene isn't how politicians and advertisers want visitors to see Glasgow, but it's as real as the porridge, and no portrait can be called beautiful unless it also includes some blemishes. Each piece here shows glimpses into many worlds inside each city. Readers may recognize some of the places our contributors describe, or they may remind them of other cities, of other places in their own minds.

JB and RG: We're grateful to all the contributors for sending such fine work to this anthology. Sincere thanks to the whole Editorial Team at Cargo Publishing, especially to Mark, Editor-in-Chief Gill Tasker who backed the project from the start, and Craig Lamont, Cargo's Design guru for making the book look so beautiful.

Thanks to Dr. Christine Neuwirth, Head of the Department of English at Carnegie Mellon University, for her enthusiasm and support, to Dr. John Lehoczky, Dean of the Dietrich College of Humanities and Social Sciences at CMU, and to the Berkman Faculty Development Fund, for underwriting the development of the enhanced electronic book. We want to thank Creative Scotland for their support, which was essential to the making of this book, also Caroline Bird, our poetry advisor for the project, and the University of Strathclyde itself, for making a significant financial contribution in the crucial early days of Second Lives.

But the special big thank you from us goes to Dr. Alistair Braidwood, who came on board at a crucial stage of the process. He is too modest to accept the praise he deserves, but he should be properly acknowledged. He brought on board all the artists from the Glasgow side, worked on the design of the book with Mark and Craig, and also took on much line to line editing work in recent months. Without him it is no exaggeration to say Second Lives would not be published at all so Ali, we both thank you.

Jane Bernstein and Rodge Glass, May 2012

Note on Grammar: this book is a collaboration between US and UK voices. In this spirit, US writers use US punctuation and spelling, UK writers use UK punctuation and spelling.

Allan Wilson | *Glasgow*

You know, it's hard to look at my own city objectively. In the same way that trying to place yourself outside your own writing and look at it from a distance is hard. When you're in it, you're in it. You live it and you can't remove yourself because then it's no longer what it was. Writing or your home city, there's not much difference – you're as much part of what makes it as it is a part of you. So I'm not sure what Glasgow means to me. It's where I've always lived and it informs my life. My family are from here and my fiancé is from here. My closest friends are from here. These things are special.

I recently drove down to Greenock. When you cross the Erskine Bridge which stretches across the River Clyde you see for miles. To your left is the City of Glasgow and to your right is the Clyde as it opens out towards the sea. The drive from Glasgow to Greenock is my favourite drive. After you cross the bridge, the road drops down to river level and there's no space between you and the water.

During this drive we went right into Greenock. It was a sunny day and we parked at the esplanade and went a walk. There was a cruise ship being loaded up and there were people on the decks. I'd never seen a boat so big. It was like looking at the pyramids. How long it must have taken to build it, how many people must have worked on it. As we walked along we noticed that there were lots of people sitting in their cars in the parking spaces along the road. There was a young couple and their kids all sitting eating bags of chips, there were old people, young people, a guy with a camera. Soon the benches began to fill up too. There must have been a few hundred people.

By the time we got back to the car we'd realised that it must have been something to do with the ship. There were two old women in the car next to us and I rolled our window down. They were eating rolls and sausage, had cups of tea in polystyrene cups. I was about to ask what was going on but Julie, my fiancé, told me they'd think we were mental or stupid at least, so we just left it. When it hit six o'clock the ship blew its horn and steam came out one of the pipes on top. Then it started to move. It was really slow. Stupidly slow. I said to Julie, if that thing is going to America or whatever it'll take fuckin four years! Tiny kids on stabilised bikes were cycling along the esplanade. Even they were going faster than the boat.

You could make out the shapes of the people on the deck. It wasn't like the Titanic, thousands of people waving or anything, they were just walking from one level to the next, going into the cabins or looking down into the water. The people on the esplanade weren't waving either. Yet everyone had turned out to see this boat take off. It made me think about my Dad's side of the family that moved to Canada in the 1960s. My Dad's Mum, My Nana, almost went. Her sister started a new life there and she was going to go with three young kids not long after my Dad's Dad died. I told Julie this story and she told me about her Nana. How when her husband died she nearly took Julie's

Mum and Uncle to Australia on a ship. They had packed all their stuff and said goodbye to the people they knew. But then on the morning they were to leave Julie's Nana couldn't do it. We spoke about all the people who must come and go everyday. Beginning new lives in different countries and the people that must do that in Glasgow. We spoke about my Mum's parents, my Gran and Grandad, who retired to the south of France. They lived there six years but when my wee brother and sister were born they came home so they could see their family grow up.

We sat in the car as the ship moved along the Clyde out to the mouth of the river then disappeared round a corner as it headed towards the sea. I thought about our life. How in a few months we'd be married and then...What? I don't know. Where will we live one day? What will we do with the time we have? Me and her, it feels like we're still just getting started. Glasgow meant nothing to me then. It didn't even enter my head. Glasgow is my city and it is part of me like I am part of it. I don't think we need each other. Glasgow will change and so will I. This city will always inform me. And when I write it is always there. But it's the other things that make it.

Remember when this was a farm?
Allan Wilson

Jamieson found a knife. It was a short and thick blade. He lifted an old newspaper from the skip and hacked at it. He jammed the point through the front until it came out the back. The blade slid downwards with ease. He walked about just holding the thing; slipping it into his belt loop then whipping it out. He pictured what he'd look like to a stranger. He rubbed it with his t-shirt to try and make it shine. On a wooden beam outside one of the houses he was able to carve his name – 'Jamieson was here'. The knife felt like it wanted to cut right through the wood.

They'd been putting up the new houses for too long. The noise would wake him in the mornings. And now that it was the spring holiday things were worse. His Mum and Dad had booked to see the show home but there was no chance he was going. He was sick of everything about the place. They'd be able to see in his bedroom window, the new people. But he wouldn't be able to see in theirs. He hated the driveways and the double garages. He hated the names of the streets: Royal Grove, Victoria Road, Windsor Crescent. He hated it all. But at least now, in its half-built state, there was still that emptiness. At the weekends when the workers were gone he could scale the fence and walk into the solitude of the place. It used to be farmers' fields. They'd stretched for miles.

At family parties he was sometimes teased by old

Aunty Jeanie who'd remind him what he used to say when he was a wee boy. "I'd ask you, 'what's on the other side of that field, pal?' And do you remember what you said? You used to put your hand up to answer, remember? Chubby arms. 'America's across there,' you'd say, 'This is Scotland and over there is America.' Remember?"

Jamieson didn't think he was that wee boy anymore. When people spoke about him being a wee boy or when they brought out photos it was like they were reminding him of someone who was dead. That was the only way he could think of it. It was quite sad sometimes thinking of it. A wee boy being dead like that. There were the home videos that his Mum would watch while he was at school. Family holidays in Majorca or Tenerife or Blackpool.

"Come and watch this," she'd say.

But he couldn't watch the things. Who were the people? Where were the people his Mum and Dad used to be? Where was the wee boy?

He slid the knife into his sock and made his way home. Some of the houses were almost up. Whole streets of them. It was a ghost town. There were dumper trucks and loose bricks. Piping and exposed wires. The blue plastic sheets that covered the walls flapped in the wind and they were the only sound. By the end of the summer the streets would be full, he knew that. Families would have moved in and his days there would be gone. There was talk of building a bigger school just to accommodate the new kids. People were saying Tesco were going to open a superstore. His Mum said she might try and get a job on the checkouts.

The clouds overhead were thick and the rain started quickly. Soon the pavements were coated and streams began to flow at the edges of the road and cascade into the drains. Jamieson sheltered in the shell of a big house. The walls and the roof were up but there was no door and he was able to walk straight in.

He hadn't been in this one before. It was the first one he'd been in that you could say was nearly ready. This one had internal walls. He walked through a doorway into a big room that he thought must be the living room. He tried to picture what it would look like with furniture and people in but it was impossible. Most of the floor was beams with the cotton wool insulation lining each square section. There were walkways with footprints across them. There was a pile of yellow overalls and hard hats in a corner near the door. The space for the windows was covered in plastic sheets but the room was still bright. There was space for sliding doors at the back. When he got to them he pulled the plastic aside and looked out to the garden. It was mostly dirt but in the soil you could see the first shoots of grass beginning to make their way to the surface. The rain soaked in, then disappeared.

It was through the door to his left that he saw it. In the room that would soon be the kitchen. There was a wall with GAS written on it in red capital letters and beneath it, in a heap, lay the animal. Jamieson shouted out. He ran away as fast as he could and by the time he was back at the entrance to the house he could feel his heart beating in his ears. He was shaking. But then, after a few seconds, he stopped. The state of him. Running away. It was the weather and the size of the house, that was all. He shook his head and began taking steps back towards the far end of the living room. He walked slowly, his head stretched out in front of the rest of his body. It was quiet except for the rain.

When he saw the animal fully he thought it was a dog. Its teeth were bared and it barked. It snapped its jaws. Jamieson stayed perched on one foot ready to make a run for it. The animal just lay there, in between the beams and the insulation, barking and hissing at him. It was a few seconds before he noticed the blood. There was a puddle around it. Splashes on the wall. He looked closer and saw how scared the animal was. He took a few more steps and the barking became frantic. The animal swinging its head from side to side but its body not moving. He'd never seen one so close like this. Never seen how red its coat was, or how orange its eyes. It was snapping at him and Jamieson held his hand out flat and made a shhh sound. It was then he saw the cubs. There were six or seven of them, hardly bigger than his hand. They were round the back of the mother, fighting each other to get to her teat. The babies didn't seem to have noticed him, or if they had they didn't care. They bounded about, leaping over one another, hopping from one side of the mother to the other, trying to find a way to her body. It was a game.

The mother was going wild and, as she snapped her jaws, some of the babies were getting nipped. When she connected they whimpered and darted away, licking the part on their body where she'd hurt them.

Jamieson held his hand out. "Here girl, good girl.

Shh." When he was only a few steps away the mother reared her head up and spat out towards him. Some of the cubs were so close he could have bent down and picked them up. Fluffy wee things. Puppy fat and flailing limbs.

"Are you hurt, girl?"

It was the first time she turned away from him. She looked to the gap that would soon become the back door. It was only a second but Jamieson looked too. The male fox was standing there, standing tall on four legs and staring at him. In its mouth was a mouse or a rat and when Jamieson faced him he dropped the food to the floor and began to bark. His teeth were bigger than the mother's. He ran forward and Jamieson jumped back. He made it out of the room then knelt down quickly and took the knife from his sock. The male had made his way over to stand in front of the mother and her babies. He was barking and sounded like a dog. Jamieson held the knife in front of his face and pointed it towards the foxes.

"I'm trying to help, okay? I can bring food. I can bring help. That's why I'm here."

Both the foxes were barking at him. Some of the cubs had run to the opposite corner and were huddled together. In two steps Jamieson was at them. The mother began to whimper. Some babies were still sucking on her teat. The father was swinging his snout and baring teeth.

Jamieson picked up one of the cubs. There was no resistance. The cub buried its head in the crevice at the bend in his arm. Teeth nibbled on his skin and it tickled.

"You both need to calm down. For God's sake."

The male picked up one of the cubs in his teeth and

made his way backwards. The mother went quiet and watched. Jamieson was at the door to the back garden and he took a step through it, the fox in one hand and the knife in the other. He turned and ran. He ran through gardens as the rain crashed down. He knocked over the wooden stakes that outlined the sections of new grass. At the end of the row of houses he turned right and was back on a street. He ran for shelter under a tree.

"You're okay boy," he said. "Everything's going to be okay."

He put the knife back in his sock and looked around. He wasn't sure what street he was on or where he was. All the streets looked the same. He kept walking in the direction he'd been running. He unzipped his jacket and put the cub next to his chest. The rain kept on. He heard thunder. The cub was quiet. Jamieson wrapped the jacket around the fox and started to run.

His Dad was at the dining table opening envelopes and his Mum was standing ironing. She turned to him and smiled.

"You're a drowned rat," she said. "Get that gear off and I'll get you a towel."

He nodded and tried to catch his breath.

His Mum stood the iron up straight and made her way towards him. "Go and get dried before you catch a chill. Don't you dare make a mess of this carpet."

When she got too close he stepped back into the porch.

"What's happened?" she said.

He saw his Dad lift his head and look over.

"What have you got in your top?" his Mum said.

He unzipped the jacket. The cub clung to his t-shirt with its claws and Jamieson turned to his Mum and smiled. He held the cub in his hand and turned it to face her.

"He followed me home, Mum."

She screamed. In the background his Dad sat for a moment, staring. He stood up slowly and made his way over.

His Mum walked back towards the wall. "It's vermin," she said.

"Let me see," his Dad said.

Jamieson held the cub beneath its arms and lifted it high.

"Give it here," his Dad said.

"Brian, you can't touch it! Get gloves! Take it outside! Throw it away!"

"Let me see it," his Dad said.

The fox hung silent in Jamieson's arms. Its paws were reaching out and when he cradled it, the fox pulled at his t-shirt.

"We could train him, Dad. Just now, when he's still a baby."

"They're wild animals," his Dad said.

"It's got diseases," his Mum said. "They carry TB!"

His Dad stopped and turned to her. "That's badgers. Badgers carry TB."

"What do foxes carry?"

"How should I know?"

"It's just a baby," Jamieson said.

His Dad held his hand out and asked again for Jamieson to hand the fox over.

"What are you going to do with him?" Jamieson said.

"Take it outside now," his Mum said. "Get it out of this house."

"We need to calm your Mum down," his Dad said.

"He's scared cos yous are screaming," Jamieson said. "He's shaking."

"Come on now pal, hand it over."

The urine was warm on Jamieson's skin. It seeped through his t-shirt and dripped down his stomach on to his jeans. He opened his arms. The fox could only grip on so long then fell to the floor and curled up on the carpet. A puddle began to form and the ends of his fur stuck together. Jamieson flicked the drips from his t-shirt, lifted the top and wiped his skin with the towel. His Dad grabbed the cub by the scruff of the neck and lifted him.

"Aw for Christ sake! Look what you've done now," his Mum said.

"If he was a dog," his Dad said, "we'd rub his face in that so he wouldn't do it again."

He held the cub at arm's length and examined it.

"I've some news for you pal. Your he is a she."

"I thought it looked like a boy."

The cub was calm in his Dad's hands.

"Don't you see what's missing?" his Dad held the fox in front of Jamieson's face.

Jamieson's Mum had retreated to the other side of the room.

"Don't make a joke of this, Brian. Get it out the house

now." She glanced at Jamieson. "Do they give you jags for tetanus in school?"

Jamieson shrugged.

"What about Rabies?"

"Go and change your top," his Dad said. "We're taking this back where you found it."

Jamieson's Dad carried the cub. They waited while a car drove past and the driver stared. Jamieson's Dad kept the animal gripped by the scruff of its neck and waved the car on. Jamieson stared down at the ground and dragged his feet.

"Where now?" his Dad said.

"There's a bit in the fence you can climb up and jump over."

"Where?"

"Over here."

Jamieson climbed it first then his Dad stretched over and handed the cub down.

"Careful in case it bites you," his Dad said. "It's not used to humans."

Jamieson took the cub and wrapped her back inside his jacket. Although it still rained it was much lighter and Jamieson and his Dad walked at normal pace.

"Don't make any sudden movements with her or she might get scared again. If she acts up then you check her. If she tries to bite, even just a nip, then you slap her nose. Got it?"

The cub didn't like it when drops of rain made their way into the jacket. She'd curl her head around and try and go within herself so that any other drops would hit the back of her neck.

"That's what you get for making me wet," Jamieson whispered.

Jamieson and his Dad walked side by side amongst the houses. At the front, where the show home was, you'd almost think it was a street people lived in. The houses had ornaments on the window sills and gardens in full bloom.

"Christ, these houses are nice," his Dad said. "We'll go and see one then you never know, eh? That could be your room right there." He pointed to a window in a house at the end of the street. "You remember when this was a farm? Look at it now."

They walked to the streets behind where houses were in various stages of the build process.

"This is like a disaster film, eh wee man? You and me and the Fantastic Mrs Fox here. The only survivors."

Every so often Jamieson felt the butt of the knife slipping in his sock and could feel the point getting caught in the hem of his jeans. He'd lean down, making sure to hold the fox tightly, and pretend to tie his laces.

"Do you want me to carry her?" his Dad asked. "If you need a break I can take her."

Jamieson shook his head. "I can't remember what house it was."

"You've got to be kidding me."

"It was raining. They all look the same."

"What street was it?"

Jamieson shrugged.

"This is called Coronation Road."

"I can't remember."

"That one there is Jubilee Gardens. Was that it?"

"It might have been, I can't remember."

"Remind me not to come to you when I lose my mind."

They continued walking down streets, turning from one into another. If he could find the skip where the knife had been then maybe he'd be able to retrace his steps.

"I've got an idea. I'll bet that she knows the way," his Dad said. "Put her down and we'll follow her. She'll be able to smell the way. That's exactly what I'm saying about them being wild. They know how to survive."

"I don't know," Jamieson said.

"Trust me," his Dad said. "If we don't find her family soon they'll move on and leave her." Jamieson took the cub from his coat and placed her on the ground. At first she just stood still then she began to pad on the spot. She put her snout to the ground then jumped straight up and sneezed.

Jamieson laughed and looked to his Dad.

"She's cute, pal, I'll give you that," his Dad said.

The cub began to walk in one direction then she turned and went the other way. Jamieson's Dad raised his eyebrows and nodded. They followed her down the street. She snaked all over the road, sniffing the odd dry patch. She took to a garden and sniffed at the dirt.

"I think this might be it," Jamieson said.

He bent down to pick up the cub and carry her inside. When his hand touched her fur she looked up at him and yelped. He tried to lift her by the neck but she snarled then bolted around the side of the house.

"Leave her," his Dad said. "This is what I mean."

"I think this is the house," Jamieson said.

They walked through the open doorway and hid Dad touched the blue plastic with his fingers.

"We should have a hat on for this," he said.

"There's some in there."

Jamieson recognised the pile of hi-vis vests in the corner. He saw the wooden walkways with his footprints smudged across them.

"They were up here," he said.

"Let me go first."

"It's fine Dad, I'm fine."

As Jamieson approached the kitchen he slowed down. He turned back to his Dad and held his finger to his lips. The foxes were there. The mother and father were looking at him, barking and growling again. Jamieson felt his Dad beside him, gripping his t-shirt at the back.

"Don't go any closer, okay? I mean it."

He thought about the knife in his pocket. How at any time, if they attacked, he would know what to do. Maybe the foxes remembered it too because they stayed back. The father was scooping up any wandering cubs in his mouth and moving them behind him and the mother.

"She's bleeding," his Dad said.

When Jamieson's cub came belting in the back door its first instinct was to run towards its mother and father. Jamieson and his Dad were looking on. The cub didn't seem to have noticed them, none of the cubs did. It was only the older foxes who sensed any danger. As the cub tried to get close to her mother, they turned and growled. The father snapped his jaws and barked at the cub. He thrust his head towards her and his teeth cut down on the cub's head. Jamieson stepped to move forward.

"Leave them," his Dad said. "It's nature."

The cub retreated while the parents directed their anger at her. They wanted space at all sides. They were backed into the corner. Jamieson and his Dad at one exit and the cub at the other.

His Dad leant in closely and whispered. "We have to go. We can't interfere."

"But I already have."

"Come on," his Dad said.

Jamieson was taken by the arm and pulled out of the room.

"They don't see her as theirs," his Dad said. "She could be a predator. They don't know she's theirs now."

Jamieson couldn't match his Dad's strength. When he could no longer see the foxes he gave in and walked beside his Dad. By the time they were at the door the crying had started.

"Eh now, come on pal. Don't do that. It's survival of the fittest. They're wild animals. Think about it, you gave that fox an experience that hardly any other foxes will ever have. Christ, it even got to meet your mother."

Jamieson couldn't stop. He wanted to get onto the street, into the rain. Above the flapping of the plastic he was sure he could hear the animals howling. He could hear their barks and their snarls and in his head he saw the animals savaging his cub. Tearing it to pieces and dishing out the remains.

"Come on now," his Dad said. "Come here wee man and give me a hug."

Jamieson eased into his dad's arms.

"That's why we're human and they're animals, wee man. That's the difference between us."

Jamieson stood back and wiped his eyes. His Dad walked towards the street then turned and waited on him. Jamieson felt for the knife in his sock. He remembered the sharpness of the steel and the way it had carved his name. He pulled it out. He held the base with both hands and heard the cub's cries from the house. He took a deep breath and turned towards the doorway as the blade flickered in the last of the day's light.

Lee Gutkind | *Pittsburgh*

The news is good—and not so good about Pittsburgh. According to the Institute for Health Metrics and Evaluation at the University of Washington, Pittsburghers are living longer than ever before--but not as long as most everyone else in the nation. Of the 67 counties in Pennsylvania, according to the County Rankings and Roadmaps report, Allegheny County, which is where Pittsburgh is located, is worst in the state for particulate matter air pollution. Allegheny County is 44th in Pennsylvania in "Health Outcomes" and 21st in "Health Factors." Allegheny County has more smokers, more obese people, more heavy drinkers, more teen births, and more STDs than elsewhere. Males born in Allegheny County in 2009 were expected to live to 75.1, compared to 76.2 nationally. Allegheny County's newborn females in 2009 were projected to live to 80.7, compared to 81.3 nationally. Single life in the city sucks, according to Forbes.com and many other surveys. And yet, according to the Washington Post's annual "in" list, Pittsburgh is in in 2012. According to National Geographic Magazine, Pittsburgh is a "must visit city" in 2012.

So even though as a single male, I am destined to be alone and to suffer a shortened lifespan, I am delighted that Pittsburgh is said to be so terrific by the outside world. Truly, I can't imagine living anywhere else.

The Miseries of Pittsburgh: Part 1
Lee Gutkind

Shadyside, Walnut Street

Tony had spotted my truck pull up outside, and now his back was to me as I waited at the counter for him to fill my cup and take my money. Like everyone at Starbucks, he knew what the regular early morning caffeine addicts drank and when, basically, we would arrive each morning. Today I am the first customer, at 6:00 a.m., on the dot, when the doors open. But it seemed, as I stood there at the counter, that filling my venti cup was taking longer than usual. And as I looked more carefully, I noticed that Tony was starting to lean backwards, then, suddenly, he was falling, ever so slowly, hovering, at first momentarily balanced in mid-air, like a lumberjack's felled tree, then gaining momentum, propelling downward. His head collided with a corner of the counter, as he crashed to the ground.

How long did I stand there, frozen, processing what had happened? Probably not more than a couple of seconds, but these moments of crisis and surprise are paralyzing. Not that I didn't know what had happened. I did. A couple of weeks before, I had arrived at Starbucks to see the ambulance pull away. It had been Tony then, too. He had had a seizure.

I walked around to the opening at the end of the

counter, once again hesitating. Should I breach the barrier and go where I did not belong to the sacred space behind the cash register and row of coffee urns, an unauthorized intruder? Of course I should. It was the right thing to do. But again, you wonder. This is a violation. Breaking an unwritten law. Customers stand in front of the cash register and employees stand behind it.

Tony was on the floor, writhing and wriggling, legs and arms, an oversized caterpillar in a Starbucks green apron. Foam bubbling from his mouth, he was emitting a gurgling noise. I could see from where I was standing, still frozen and unsure if I should breach the barrier, that his hair around his scalp was soaked with blood. What to do? If another customer came into the store and saw me kneeling down behind the cash register hovering over a bloody Tony, what might they think?

Meredith, who worked early morning shift with Tony, came out of the storage room carrying a tray of supplies. "Oh, My God," she said, spotting Tony.

I wanted to say, "He's had a seizure." But I couldn't think of the word "seizure," I was so nervous. So I said fit. "He's had a fit."

She stared at me, nodding. She understood, but she wasn't moving.

"Meredith, he's bleeding," I said.

She's a college student, in her early twenties, quiet and bookish. When she learned about my new book, my memoir, in the fall of last year, she was the first person I knew who went to the library to take it out and read it. Not long before, I gave a reading at the University of Pittsburgh where I once taught, and she was there.

Meredith," I said. "Call 911."

She picked up the phone.

Her movement to the phone suddenly released me. Finally, I breached the barrier, dashing around the pastry display, kneeling down and cupping Tony's bloody head in my hand.

Leadership Pittsburgh

Bob O'Connor was mayor of the city of Pittsburgh during that time. He was Irish Catholic, but fell in love with an orthodox Jewish woman, Judy Levine, with whom he eloped to Wheeling, West Virginia.

O'Connor had thick, wavy silver hair, his trademark, and, among other jobs before entering politics and working his way up through the democratic machine to the presidency of city council and mayor, he managed restaurants specializing in fried chicken and fast food burgers. Tom Murphy was the mayor before Bob O'Connor. He was Irish and had silver hair, not as full as O'Connor's, however, and, over his three terms in office, Murphy led the city of Pittsburgh into bankruptcy. Murphy also nearly singlehandedly engineered the potential sale of the National League's Pittsburgh Pirate franchise to cable TV franchise owner John J. Rigas, who was arrested and jailed for corruption, in time for the city to bail out of the deal.

Tom Flaherty, Irish, has been Controller, the city's chief financial officer. His slogan when he ran for office as Judge of Common Pleas Court in 2005 was "Good controller . . . good judge." He was elected. His final recommendation upon leaving office was to abolish the position of Controller in which he had served for 16 years.

Pete Flaherty was, like Tom Flaherty and Bob O'Connor, first a City Councilman and Irish, then a two-term-mayor, followed by three more terms as an Allegheny County Commissioner. He had long wavy hair, dark, not silver, but good hair, anyway. Pittsburgh is the major metropolitan area in Allegheny County, population 1.2 million. The leaders of the county and the leaders of the city are almost always at odds. You can count on their good hair, though.

James Flaherty, Pete's brother, was a County Commissioner during that period—elected a few years after Pete. There were three County Commissioners at any one time in office. Shawn Flaherty, Pete's son, ran for county sheriff in 2002 and lost, but subsequently won a special election to become a State Representative when his predecessor, Jeff Habay, resigned after pleading no contest to 21 charges, including theft and violations of the state Ethics Act, and send to jail. He lost his pension.

Tom Flaherty's Controller counterpart in Allegheny County was Mark Patrick Flaherty who is the son of James Flaherty and nephew of Pete Flaherty. James Flaherty is now a Commonwealth of Pennsylvania Court judge. Chelsa Wagner is the current County Controller, while Jack Wagner, her uncle is Pennsylvania State Auditor General and Eileen Wagner, her aunt, was County Register of Wills. Chelsa's father and her grandfather were district Magistrates. A magistrate is a minor judicial officer, kind of like a low-rent judge.

Ben Woods, another former president of Pittsburgh City Council served four years in jail for tax evasion, but when released from the federal penitentiary, became an official in the Allegheny County Democratic party, working with Tom Murphy, O'Connor and the Flahertys.

Cyril Wecht, the prestigious forensic pathologist, a frequent guest on Larry King Live and other network TV news shows, who added his expertise to the John F. Kennedy assassination and the O.J. Simpson trial, had been an Allegheny County Coroner and Commissioner, as well as Chairman of the Democratic party. In 2005, Wecht was charged in an 84-counts indictment for mail and wire fraud, theft and the illegal trading of unclaimed bodies with a local Catholic college.

Among high-profile cases in which federal prosecutors said Cyril Wecht fraudulently billed clients using Allegheny County facilities for private consulting were the manslaughter trial of former NBA star Jayson Williams and the California murder trial of Scott Peterson, accused of killing his wife Laci and their unborn son. After a long and complicated trial, Wecht was acquitted.

Cyril Wecht's son, a former employee of his father's private pathology practice, is Pennsylvania Superior Court Judge David Wecht.

Sophie Masloff, a Jewish grandmother with a high school education, became President of City Council while Cyril Wecht was County Commissioner, when her predecessor, Louis Mason, died. A few years later, when Mayor Richard Caliguiri died, Sophie Masloff became

Mayor. She ran for re-election two years later, campaigning with the slogan inspired by William Styron, "Sophie's Choice—a Clean City."

No one could understand the reason Sophie used the book about another Sophie, who was a fictional Holocaust survivor, as a campaign figure and slogan, especially since the book took place in Brooklyn. But there were Sophie's Choice posters all around the city, even on the public trash cans and garbage trucks. Sophie was re-elected.

Twenty three year old Luke Ravenstahl, a graduate of North Catholic High School, was elected to City Council in 2003. His work experience after college, where he played football, was as an account manager for a courier service. His grandfather was a Pennsylvania state representative and his dad, Robert, a District Magistrate, like Chelsa's father and grandfather.

In 2006, Luke Ravenstahl, became President of Pittsburgh's City Council when the council was deadlocked over leadership, and gave the position to Ravenstahl as a compromise move. It made sense to the veteran members of City Council, who wanted no part of the extra administrative responsibilities Council President incurred. Give it to the young kid who was too dumb to realize he was being suckered.

A few months later, when O'Connor suddenly died, Ravenstahl became Mayor—this was the path of succession—and Luke was suddenly the youngest and most inexperienced mayor of a major metropolitan city, ever.

In 2009, State Senator Jane Orie, from McCandless Township, a Pittsburgh suburb, was charged, along with her sister and administrative assistant, Janine Orie, of using her legislative staff and resources to run re-election campaigns for their elder sister, a Pennsylvania Commonwealth State Judge, Joan Orie Melvin.

In 2010, Adam Ravenstahl, Luke's brother, was elected to the Pennsylvania House of representatives. In 2011, Corry O'Connor, 27, Bob O'Connor's son, was elected to Pittsburgh City Council.

The beat goes on.

Theresa Heinz, the former wife of Senator John Heinz, who died in a 1991 helicopter and plane collision, and her current husband Massachusetts Senator John Kerry have a house in Pittsburgh, but since the 2004 presidential election in which Kerry was defeated by George W. Bush, they rarely visit.

Eggs

Mornings before driving three minutes to Starbucks at 5:55 a.m., I place three eggs in a pot of water and turn on the fire. When I return from Starbucks I check on the eggs and then climb up to the second floor to begin to write or answer e-mail. At that point I remind myself to return to the eggs in 10 minutes because the pot I use is very small and the water boils away quickly, if I don't pay attention. But I always seem to forget about the eggs in the pot on those mornings, and at some point invariably I hear the "pop" "pop" "pop" as the eggs explode across the room.

Wisdom

William Styron, whose work inspired Sophie's re-election slogan, taught me that the prostrate makes all men equal.

Styron, the author of "The Confessions of Nat Turner" and, among other brilliant books, "Sophie's Choice," is in town to give a Saturday evening reading at a conference. His agent picks him up at the airport late Friday night and takes him directly to a party at Chuck Kinder's house. Kinder is a novelist who teaches at the University of Pittsburgh. He's also the model for his student's, Michael Chabon's, hapless character in the book and movie Wonderboys, played by Michael Douglas.

Although born in Washington, D.C., Chabon is basically a hometown boy, raised in the Squirrel Hill, Shadyside and Oakland sections of the city. These are basically the cultural and intellectual districts where the university professors, the doctors and lawyers and CPAs live. Pittsburgh is very much a neighborhood kind of place. We've got our Little Italy, our Jewish quarter, our black ghettos and our manicured suburban WASP retreats, including the aptly named, Fox Chapel, where polo is a popular past time.

Chabon's first book, a coming of age tale, was well received, published in 1988 when he was only 25, entitled The Mysteries of Pittsburgh. It was Chabon's first novel, which he began writing when he was an undergraduate at the University of Pittsburgh. In 2008 it was made into a major motion picture, filmed in the city, in Shadyside where Tony had his seizure and Squirrel Hill where Kinder's party took place.

Chabon actually left town before the Mysteries of Pittsburgh were published, but that is not unusual. Pittsburgh is overloaded with families of famous people who once lived here and don't anymore. Rob Marshall, Annie Dillard, David McCullough, Dan Marino, are rooted in Pittsburgh. Jeff Goldblum even made a movie in Pittsburgh about returning to town to visit, although he didn't stay long.

Exploding Penis

Styron's agent's family lives in the city, so she makes Styron's appearance a tax-deductible reason to weekend here. He's a charming southern gentleman with wavy white hair and an unpretentious formality. He drinks and chats with the women, mostly, at Kinder's party, and we close the party down. In my car, heading for this hotel, he suddenly remembers that he has forgotten to retrieve his luggage from his agent's car. Worse, his agent uses her married name; he doesn't know her family name so we can't look it up in the phonebook. The information operator is not helpful. When we telephone her home phone in Washington where she lives, thinking that maybe her husband will provide the necessary information, we get an answering machine.

Now we are riding around in the car, late Friday night turning into early Saturday morning. The roads are empty, the bars and restaurants long past closing, the city dark and dead.

"We'll go to a convenience store, and you can get what you need for the night—an extra toothbrush, stuff like that," I said.

"But my prostate medicine was in that suitcase."

For a second, I don't get what Styron is telling me.

"It's not brushing my teeth I am worrying about," Styron told me. "I need to pee. In fact," he hesitated. "I will need to pee soon." Then he added, for emphasis: "Very soon."

I am sitting in my car in the dark in the middle of my home-town, a down-on-its-ass city with a shrinking population, a dwindling tax-base and a disintegrating infrastructure, with the great Pulitzer-prize winning author, William Styron, a friend of Hillary and Bill Clinton, Jesse Jackson and God knows who else—superstars, world leaders. To me, this was incredible.

For months, I had looked forward to this weekend so that I could momentarily rub elbows with Styron and perhaps in some way gain wisdom and insight into his greatness. Not that I thought that his brilliance would rub off on me and I would become a better writer, a more acknowledged national presence. But something.

What I learned was that William Styron needs to pee on a regular basis, just like me. This is the great equalizer—the nitty-gritty bare-basic essential that brings us all together. All men need to pee. But I am better than Styron in that regard. I can pee at will.

As we sat in the emergency room that night in the local hospital where I had taken him for his medicine, chatting about the Clinton White House, Charles and Diana and the other swell people with whom he hung out, I thought back to another pre-eminent author I had once hosted at a similar conference, the great Nelson Algren, author of the "Man with the Golden Arm."

When he was asked what, if anything, he wanted to do during a free afternoon in Pittsburgh before his evening program, he replied: "I want to go to a department store. I need to buy some underwear."

So much for the larger than life figures and the glitter and aura of fortune and fame.

Millergate

Sienna Miller's character in the movie version of Mysteries of Pittsburgh is an alluring classical violinist named Jane Bellwether. Like her character, Miller in person, is compelling and straightforward and very pretty—downright glamorous. And just like the Flahertys and the Ories and so many others, she has Pittsburgh connections. Miller's father, Edward Miller, a banker, lives in Crawford County, north of Pittsburgh and not far from where the actress Sharon Stone grew up, which is close enough to Pittsburgh for the newspapers to mention every time her name is in the news. In Pittsburgh if you have local connection, you are anointed. Rarely can a locally connected person do wrong—until Sienna Miller.

Sienna Miller had another local connection, very special: The then 26-year-old boy-mayor of Pittsburgh and former courier company supervisor, Luke Ravenstahl. They met at party and Luke, whose marriage to his high school sweetheart was currently unraveling, may have been dumbstruck with love. It was Luke who spoke on Miller's behalf one day in 2006, accepting her apology and begging Pittsburghers to forgive Sienna, while at the same time imploring her to give the city a chance—and to maybe give him a chance, too.

The incident occurred in an interview with Rolling Stone when Sienna complained to a reporter about the difficult life of being a movie star, saying, "Can you believe this is my life?" Will you pity me when you're back in your funky New York apartment and I'm still in . . .

Now wait.

It is difficult to know exactly what was going through Sienna's mind as she was being interviewed. Maybe she had had a bad day. Or maybe she wanted to say something to intrigue or incite or maybe inflame the boy Mayor. Or maybe it just slipped out—a mistake. But whatever the source or the truth of her intent on that day when interviewed by Rolling Stone, she made a fatal error.

She meant to say "Pittsburgh" when she was talking about her awful movie star plight in life and the reporter was back in his funky apartment. However, Sienna Miller said "Shitsburgh"

Which is allright. Sienna didn't have to like Pittsburgh as much as Luke did or Sophie did or even as much as William Styron. But her frustrated outburst didn't help the movie too much or the burgeoning film industry in town. You don't diss Pittsburgh while you are in Pittsburgh. The Burghers will hunt you down. Never forget.

A few days later, Miller apologized, explaining that

because of her work schedule, she only saw the city at night. She was certain to change her mind in daylight.

First Monday

Deer hunting is a sacred tradition of the blue-collar community in western Pennsylvania and a rite of passage for kids growing up here, not unlike a bar mitzvah. You join the men on "First Monday"--that's the Monday after Thanksgiving, usually the first Monday in December--when you are old enough to get a hunting license, which is twelve in Pennsylvania, where two hundred thousand white-tail deer are harvested annually. Today was a Sunday in September, a day before the first Monday of archery season, an excuse for me and my friends to get out of the city and away from job and family for a long weekend, looking for signs of deer in preparation for the real first Monday--the Monday when guns are allowed--a couple of months away.

From a sportsman's point-of-view, you do not kill deer; rather, you "harvest" the biggest and oldest animals because of a dearth of vegetation in the forest for the multiplying whitetail herd to consume. Bucks--those deer with antlers, which hunters call "bone"--are the object of the hunt on first Monday. By eliminating the big strong male who, due to size, strength and experience controls the food supply, the lives of younger, weaker members of the herd, who might otherwise starve, are spared.

Around Christmas, a second "harvest" occurs: doe season; doe are quite plentiful and easier to ambush. The idea in deer hunting is to sneak into the woods at about 4 a.m., conceal yourself--some hunters climb trees--and wait, often in sub-zero temperatures, for first light when the deer wake up and start foraging for food. You need to sit very still so as not to give yourself away, and to be down-wind of your prey, because deer are very sensitive to smell and sound. The philosophy in deer hunting is total ambush. When you ambush and kill your first deer, you are considered a man.

I have yet to make that passage, not because I was against killing deer or that I hadn't tried to harvest a buck; rather, I was much more interested in why other people invested so much time and energy killing an animal they would often decline to eat. On first Monday, I would usually wait for first light and then, if there were no deer directly in my line of fire, I would get up (or climb down if I am in a tree) and walk around, looking for other hunters to talk with, usually those who had already killed their buck and had nothing better to do than hang it from a tree and wait for onlookers to examine their prey and ask for shot-by-shot details.

Walking along the side of a road one first Monday, I met a woman hauling a seven-point (the number of single antlers or "bone" on a buck) in the bed of her pick-up truck. She shot the buck in the left temple--she shoved her pinky finger into the tiny hole below the animal's eye to show me--with a single shot from her 30-06 at 100 yards, she said. Deer hunters have a keen sense of distance. In the field where the deer lay dead, she slit open it's stomach with a Buck knife, pulled out it's innards, lashed it's bone with a rope and then dragged it along the ground to her truck. At home, she would hang the deer from the supporting beam of her front porch so that at the end of the day, when her neighbors rode by in their pick-up trucks, they'd witness her success.

WWMG

After my divorce some years ago, I went to see a psychiatrist, whom I will call Dr. Mason. When I walked into his office, I thought that he looked familiar, and I said so. But we didn't dwell on the subject—I was deeply hurt by my first wife, feeling abandoned, afraid of being alone—and I needed to talk with someone--fast. Two years later, we were still talking.

I'm not sure if Dr. Mason was a great psychiatrist or if I was finally ready to confront my problems, but the transformation that occurred in me was phenomenal. I had never been able to express my feelings—one of the reasons for the failure of my marriage. Throughout my life, I had been seething with anger, inherited from my father, who had been abused as a child and, subsequently, abusive to me.

Equally damaging was the neighborhood where I grew up, which was sharply divided by class and religion. I had the religion right—Jewish—but my father worked in a shoe store, while most of the families around us were populated by professionals—physicians, attorneys and so on. To make matters worse, I was grossly overweight. The boys at school called me Slim.

All of these pressures came to a head when I transferred from the small neighborhood school in Greenfield,
Roosevelt School, that I had been attending to the large
high school, Taylor Allderdice, where status divisions
were glaringly apparent. Because I was Jewish and fat,
the kids from the "wrong" side of the tracks used me as
their whipping boy. Because we were not country club
types, the wealthy kids, mostly Jewish—the group to
which I thought I belonged—ignored me. Sensing that I
had been deeply wounded by this lack of identity and opportunity to bond, Dr. Mason bypassed discussion of my
divorce and persuaded me to go back in time and relive the
roots of my alienation.

One of our sessions was especially revelatory. I was
attempting to relate an incident that had occurred when
I was 13 years old, an incident so hurtful that I had been
unable to remember it all at once at any one moment.
Whenever I started thinking about it--and I found myself
re-living snatches regularly--I would shut it down before
it became too threatening to endure. But that day, it all
came back.

I was sitting at my desk in school when suddenly
the boys—the wealthy Jewish boys—began parading into
the room, en-masse, grinning sheepishly, and displaying
the uniform they were wearing: Khaki pants and blue
and white crew-neck sweatshirts with four bold initials
WWMG—and the words corresponding to the letters-
-Work-Wisdom-Morality-Goodness.

To that moment, I had honestly hoped that, over a
period of time, I could become a part of this in-group,

with whom I had worked hard to befriend. But I knew that these sweat-shirted boys had clearly defined their separateness and closed off their circle of intimacy without me--forever. I felt an awful, sinking, empty feeling that has lingered with me to this day. I assumed then that I would always be alone, vulnerable to abandonment, and from that point on, I had acted that way, with hostility to many people, never trusting anyone.

Reliving this image in Dr. Mason's office, I realized something else—that I recognized and remembered one of those WWMG boys from a different time and place. He was heavyset then, with a full head of hair and no eyeglasses, and in fact, he had a different name. But there was no question that one of the WWMG boys who had trooped into that room and marked me as an outcast was the man I now knew as Dr. Mason. "You were there," I said. He admitted it.

"You ruined my life."

I was being overly dramatic—and we both knew it—but I was shocked and disappointed. Had he remembered me from the very beginning and led me on—in order to collect his fees and to embarrass me? I knew that wasn't true; the realization that we had a history probably came to him the same time it came to me; yet, doubt and paranoia were unavoidable. And why was his name was different? "I had my reasons," he said when I confronted him. After that, I was silent and confused.

What do you do when you find out that your psychiatrist might be an imposter or a fraud—and a former enemy?

I have to say that I did not devote a lot of time to answering that question because I decided, quickly, that it didn't matter. What seemed to matter is that I had been able to trust and confide in someone, and because of that bond, I had learned things about the reasons behind my actions and motivations that, over the previous years, had totally eluded and damaged me.

So if Dr. Mason was an imposter—if he had betrayed me—then what of it? I had survived. Nothing bad happened, except that I gained special insight and awareness of the forces that had shaped me. Bottom line, I had significantly benefited from his therapy. I could yell and scream and then quit working with him and find an other therapist, and I think that that's exactly what I would have done two years before—erupted in a tantrum, stormed out of his office, convinced that I could never rely on anyone, even a shrink.

One afternoon, seven years later, I announced to Dr, Mason that I didn't think I needed to work with him anymore. At the end of that session, we stood up and, for the first time since our first meeting, shook hands. "Is there anything else you want to ask or say?" he said.

There was, of course—and there always would be. But I didn't then—and I probably never will.

Revenge of the Kike

I saw Johnny Duncan a few years after high school when I was driving down Murray Avenue in Pittsburgh, where I grew up, not far from the Homestead Steel Works. Johnny was sitting on the steps of a bar called the Coop, smoking and drinking beer, with a couple of other guys, drunk and disheveled and surly. He looked me right in the eye as I cruised passed, and I can still hear what he said then, loudly: "Kike."

Johnny Duncan and I knew each other because we both went to Roosevelt elementary school at around the same time. Roosevelt was located in the Greenfield section of Pittsburgh, the 15th Ward. This was important, moreso to me, than to Johnny, I suspect. If I had lived in the 14th Ward, literally a few blocks from my house, I would be in the Squirrel Hill section, which was where most of the Jews in the city then lived—and many very wealthy people, not surprisingly. If I had lived in Squirrel Hill I would have gone to Linden School or Colfax School, where the Jews were the majority and kike was anathema. If I had lived in Squirrel Hill I could have also played little league baseball with kids I wanted to meet and to whom I thought I could relate. I once tried out and was selected to be on a Little League team in the 14th Ward, but when my 15th Ward identity was discovered, I was cut. As it turned out, I could not relate to those Squirrel Hill kids, anyway; in the long run, I related moreso to the Greenfield culture, although they, as Johnny demonstrated, did not relate to me.

Johnny was short, wiry and brooding; he never said much in class and remained at the social fringes. We were kindred spirits in that respect, for I too was a loner, but from totally incompatible sides of the tracks—at lest symbolically. I can't remember ever having a conversation with him.

Greenfield was primarily Catholic blue-collar section where many of my classmates parents worked in the mills— J&L Steel, US Steel, Mesta Machine, multi-million dollar Trojan Horses, gone and forgotten now, although many of my classmates ended up there for a while, witnessing their decline and disappearance. The few Jewish kids in Greenfield usually caught up with the Squirrel Hill kids at Taylor Allderdice High School (Now called Pittsburgh Allderdice) or in college and went on to grad school, med school, law school, ignoring their Greenfield roots—at least for a while. It was the unwritten rule—a tacit understanding around the neighborhood—that you denigrate, beat up on the college-bound boys because they'd be back in the neighborhood ten years later, doctors, accountants and attorneys, beating up on you by squeezing your pocketbooks dry.

This in essence is the meaning of the word, "kike:" Someone who is shrewd, dishonest—and Jewish. So, according to most dictionaries and most anti-Semites, Johnny's disdain is well founded. But according to Leo Rosten, in THE JOYS OF YIDDISH, "kike" was first used on Ellis Island, when mostly illiterate Jewish immigrants refused to sign entry-forms with an "X," which was symbolic of the crucifix and the horrors of their Christian oppressors. Instead, they used an "O"; the Jewish word for circle is "kikel." So "kike" was not at first meant as a denigrating racial term.

My family members were not anything like those alleged bloodsuckers the Greenfield boys fixated on. My parents had no money to send me to college. Why else would we live in Greenfield, if we could have afforded better? This shabby rundown corner of a once vital and now dying industrial center was no place for the Chosen people. And I, classic Greenfield underachiever, very much like those boys hanging out at The Coop, scraped my way out of high school, barely graduating at the fifth fifth of my class. After high school, I went into the military. That time when Johnny called me a kike, I had just mustered out and I was living at home trying to decide what to do for the next act of my life.

Had it been one of the Greenfield boys who had terrorized me—those tough kids who waited to beat on me as I walked up the steps at school, morning and afternoon—I might have stopped my car and demonstrated what I had learned in the military about attack, but I had no bad history with or resentment of Johnny Duncan. I let it pass-- and have regretted letting it pass up until today.

Forty or so years later, I am at Ritter's Diner with my 12-year-old son, Sam, where we breakfast almost every morning, sitting at the counter in almost the same place we always sit. There are many other regulars at Ritter's, people I have seen for half dozen years and have passed the time of day with. But I have never said a word to Johnny Duncan, though we often sit beside one another at the counter, nearly touching shoulders. Ritter's is a Pittsburgh Institution. Art Velisaris co-owns Ritter's Diner with his brothers George, Orestis and Pete. Soups, pies, home fries and the rest are made on-premises. So is the gravy that's used on the diner's most popular entrees--meat loaf and hot roast beef sandwiches.

I think the world has not treated Johnny Duncan too well. He seems sad and lonely, looks old and beaten; he lingers over his coffee for long periods, staring off into space, smoking cigarette after cigarette. He is stockier than I remember and his hair is thick gray. His face is gray, too, and deeply creased. At Ritter's we look through one another.

But I remember the tail end of a conversation I overheard about a year ago between Johnny and a waitress. "So I am waiting for the results," Johnny said. And the waitress, surprised by the intimacy of the admission, looked away when he added, whispering, "I'm scared."

I moved closer to Sam, wondering why Johnny had no one else to talk with and confess to, except the clearly startled Ritter's waitress.

But today I saw Johnny again for the first time since I overheard that conversation. He's not been to Ritter's for at least a year, or not at the regular time when I would see him. He looks older, even grayer, walks a little slower now. But he lingered over his coffee and cigarettes same as before, staring in silence out into space.

"Anyway," he told a waitress, stopping her as she walked by, "the doctors are hopeful. The tests are looking good."

The waitress nodded perfunctorily, but added: "I am happy to hear that."

"I have my embarrassing moments," he added. "You know?" he said.

She nodded.

"I'll see you later," Johnny Duncan told her a little later, as he downed his coffee and snubbed a butt. "I will let you know."

When he walked away from the counter to pay his check, I noticed that Johnny had a big white puffy parcel stuffed halfway into his back pocket.

"What's that white thing?" Sam asked.

"It's a diaper," I said.

"Why is that man carrying a baby diaper?" asked Sam.

"I think he is sick."

That day so long ago when Johnny Duncan, sitting on the stoop at The Coop, called me "kike" is engrained into my memory. I will never forget the rush of anger and humiliation I experienced—and the hopelessness of blind and ignorant prejudice. And I will never forget also the fact that I never saw Johnny again after that day of his conversation with the waitress, even though Sam and I return to Ritter's regularly.

But, alas, my memory has gaps.

Eggs

Once again, I have forgotten the eggs I have been boiling on the stove in the kitchen as I have been writing this. I've been to Starbucks on Walnut for my Venti. I've put the eggs in the pot, turned on the burner and promised myself to remember. "Don't forget the eggs. Don't forget the eggs," I repeated to myself.

First came the sickeningly familiar, "pop" "pop",

"pop." And then as I ran downstairs, the smoke detector detonated and the noise engulfed the house: "Bleep, bleep, bleep."

I extinguished the burner and opened the kitchen door and waited until the stench was gone and the smoke alarm reset. Then I went back up to Starbucks for a second Venti.

What's with these eggs? Why am I always forgetting?

Lori Jakiela | *Pittsburgh*

When I was a kid, I traveled with my father every weekend to see my grandfather in Braddock, a mill town outside of Pittsburgh proper. My grandfather, an immigrant, spoke only Polish. My father believed in America, the dream of it. "We speak American in my house," he said. We had a Chrysler Newport, a car as big as a meat locker. We vacationed in Florida. My father played the lottery and had a bookie. "We speak American," he said. He kept to that until just before he died. Then his brain turned on him and went back to its first language and my father spent his last conscious hours trying to tell me something I couldn't understand. "Nonsense," my uncle said, and refused to translate. I still don't believe my uncle. I think my father was trying to tell me something that would make the world and everything in it make sense.

On those drives to Braddock, we passed under the George Westinghouse Bridge, a massive span that rose above The Electric Valley. Westinghouse had an electric plant there. From the bridge, you could see the fire of the Edgar Thompson Works, the mill where the men from my father's family worked at one time or another. "That's the bridge to take when things get serious," my mother, a nurse who worked for years in Braddock, used to say, a joke, meaning that was the bridge most chosen by suicides for its height, its lack of water underneath. There were bodies in the concrete, workers buried in the bridge itself. People died there. "In service to mankind," the message on the bridge's monument reads.

That bridge to take when things get serious.

That's my Pittsburgh, my way of seeing.

Working the Red Eye, Pittsburgh to Vegas
Lori Jakiela

The man in the emergency exit row has been drinking
from his own bottle of duty-free vodka
and because he was quiet about it,
kept his clothes on, and didn't hit
his call button even once
no one notices until we land in Vegas
and he refuses to get off the plane.

He's sure we haven't gone anywhere.
 "You people think I'm a sucker," he says.
"I'm no sucker. I paid good money for this."
He boarded in Pittsburgh, my home country.
In Pittsburgh, we have two dreams:
to go to Vegas to live
and to go to Florida to die.

The gate agents call the police.
The pilots are pissed.
The A-line flight attendant with the fake French name
twirls a pair of plastic handcuffs and says,
"These make me so-o-o hot."

My father, who stopped drinking years ago
but never found his way, loved Vegas.
He'd carry a sweatsock full of good-luck
nickels through security

and get stopped every time.
He died at home in a rented hospital bed
in Pittsburgh, not Florida.

"Sir," I say to the drunk on the plane
who squeezes his eyes shut so he doesn't have to see me.
"Please put your shoes on."

"Fuck you," he says. "I'm not going anywhere."

No Amount of Money Can Get You a Better Coke
Than The One the Bum on the Corner is Drinking

It's the most popular drink in the sky, more popular
than champagne. The great equalizer, Andy Warhol
called Coke, the drink of a democracy.
"The President drinks Coke, Liz Taylor drinks Coke,
and just think, you can drink Coke, too," Andy said
to explain why he painted it.

Andy Warhol was from my hometown. Pittsburgh.
All working-class grit.
Andy's family ran a junkyard in Carrick.
His real name was Warhola.
He didn't like to admit that.
He liked to say he was from New York.
He liked to say he was a robot.

Diet Coke cuts through anything.

After a bird strike, pilots ask for Diet Coke
to clean blood and feathers off the windshield.

Mill Hunk

When he was young, my father sang
on the radio in Braddock.
He cut a record and dreamed of Broadway,
sleek suits, silver boxes of fat cigars, the best
bourbon. He sang "Begin the Beguine," a song
Cole Porter wrote drunk at the Paris Ritz.
"Begin the Begin," my father called it,
in the years before he got married.

Then he grew up, wised up, buckled down.
He worked in the mills. "Face reality,"
he said. "This isn't a dream world."
Even after he retired he wore work clothes.
His skin showed through shirts
stained black with graphite.

"I can never remember it,"
Cole Porter said of that song.

Machine

My father was a machinist,
but when I was very young
I thought the word
was machine.
This was a joke he told for years.

Sometimes he would bring home
presents from work –
bits of steel and springs
in his pockets.

Here, he'd say,
Go make something beautiful.

Kapka Kassabova | *Glasgow*

Eduard Bersudsky, drawings 1968-71

The Organ Grinder
Kapka Kassabova

'People are killed for poetry here – a sign of unparalleled respect –
because they are still capable of living by it.' – Osip Mandelstam

Glasgow pulls you under like a rip in the current. You walk
down a side street and end up thirty years back in time.
The rain is like acid on your face. You walk down a side
street, and shop fronts slap you. Buildings end suddenly,
as if sliced with a knife. Every time you look up from the
red brick and concrete, the sky falls like a lid over you.
You walk down a side street and into a place called Trans-
Europe Café where the mustard chairs remind you of your
kindergarten, and the round plastic clocks show the time
in Berlin's Alexander Platz, 1984, when you visited with
your parents because Berlin was as far west as you could
go. Later you stood by the Wall eating sandwiches with
gherkins, avoiding your parents' eyes. The sadness and
the resignation in their eyes. They were exactly the age
you are now. You order a Trans-Europe sandwich from the
Polish waitress. You struggle to remain calm. If you lived
here, you'd become deranged.

But you don't live here, and anyway it's not Glasgow's fault. You already carry the derangement with you,
ever since you left the city of your youth. The derangement is called Socialist Realism.

Until the day the Berlin Wall fell, catapulting you

and your parents to a sudden new destiny called emigration, Sofia lived in the shadow of chestnut trees and late totalitarianism. It was criss-crossed with tinkling trams and punctuated by old churches, but high above soared the big-fisted proletarian monuments of the Bright Future and the concrete high-rises where you grew up, imagining you were somewhere else, somewhere in the pages of Evgenii Onegin and Call of the Wild. The giant red star on the neo-classical façade of the Communist Party HQ looked kind of rusty. As your mother – who liked reading Montaigne, Remarque, and Dostoevsky – spent her days instead queuing up for whatever was in the shops (Cuban oranges, red boots for you and your sister), the sun-bleached portraits of Marx and Lenin looked down on her with disdain. She was not an individual – individualism was the sin of the decadent West – she was a cog in the great machine of the future. 'PROLETARIANS OF THE WORLD, UNITE!' the faded banner between Marx and Lenin urged, but the citizens of Sofia had stopped looking up decades ago. They were too busy queuing. Those who liked books, like my mother and me, practiced 'internal emigration', which meant that in their heads they pretended they were somewhere else. Somewhere without Party HQs, without concrete high-rises, without proletarian monuments, and definitely without a Bright Future. Somewhere individualistic and decadent.

Now it's twenty three years since the Wall fell, you have moved countries three times, own three passports, live in near-by Edinburgh, and you walk down a Glasgow side-street. You see a union-led strike, except a strike here is called 'industrial action'. People in brown jackets are protesting about public sector pensions being cut back. Fair enough, public sector pensions here are generous so you can understand why they're protesting; then you see a flag with a hammer and sickle.

It's sleeting, and darkness falls at noon. You don't want to be here, but you walk down a side-street because you are looking for something today. They are expecting you. It must be somewhere here, among Terry's Tattoo Studio, City Centre Smile Studio (Open Saturday's), Scotsmann Models, The Treasure Bunker, and Russian Café Cossachok. Here it is.

You climb the stairs and knock on the heavy door signed 'Sharmanka Kinetic Theatre'. It's dark inside, perhaps they've forgotten you were coming. After all, you've never met before. The door opens with a creak.

Tatyana Jakovskaya wears a baggy black dress under which the contours of her body loom like a mountain range.

'Ah, Kapka, is this you?' She smiles behind big glasses. 'Come in. Sit down. I'll make tea.' Tatyana's accent drips with raw treacle, it's so heavy. Tatyana is your mother's age. She invites you to sit at a hand-carved table with round edges, and disappears at the back.

It's cavernous and chilly inside the hall. You have stepped into another dimension. All around you larger-than-life mechanical toys stare with bug eyes and wood-carved faces. Harlequins hang upside down and monkeys leer. Everywhere, the shadows of saints and sinners, despots and donkeys, rats and ravens that ring alarming little bells. Wheels and clogs sit silent in infernal mechanisms only a button switch away. This is a kinetic theatre – the door sign says so – but it is also something else, because theatres feel safe and here, you are in the midst of something big, true, and utterly unconsoling. What exactly is Sharmanka?

Sharmanka is the Russian word for barrel organ, a mechanical music device which arrived in Russia a long time ago with the breezy popular tune 'Charmante Catherine', hence the name.

Sharmanka is the love child of émigrés Tatyana Jakovskaya, a theatre director, and Eduard Bersudsky, a sculptor and artist who presently emerges from the back with mugs of tea. He is a distracted man with white hair and a shuffle. He puts a tea mug before you, with a plate of lemon slices.

'Kapka. In Russian, Kaplja. Dewdrop. You take honey?' He shuffles away again.

Sharmanka is where Tatyana and Eduard live in a couple of cramped rooms at the back, like Parisian bohemians in the 1930s. One of the rooms is Eduard's workshop, where the entrails of Glasgow are arranged in cabinet draws labelled in Russian: bolts; coils; springs; clocks; bells. The other is the kitchen. Vegetables wait in a bowl for tonight's borscht. You are too embarrassed to ask where they sleep.

Back in the theatre hall, Eduard spoons honey into your tea-mug. One, two, three spoons... He can't stop. Eduard is not a man of moderation. Once, he stopped speaking – for two years. Why? Tatyana shakes her head. Eduard shrugs. Perhaps he had nothing to say with words. He was busy building things with broken bits of furniture and smuggled electrical plugs, in his tiny bedroom in a communal Leningrad flat. In Soviet Russia all flats were communal, to demonstrate the triumph of Socialist Realism over all things bourgeois, starting with ownership and ending with privacy. Eduard – who wasn't a member of the state-approved Union of Artists – was building things that no one could see because they were ideologically and aesthetically wrong. Things like 'The Clock of Life' which Tatyana switches on for you now.

Lights come on, an invisible curtain opens, bells toll for all of us, and a symphony of carved figures explodes into life. The cycle of life and death rotates before you in carved scenes: a woman embraces a boy-child who grows up and has a woman and a child, then grows old, and is embraced by Death. And then the wheel turns again. And then another wheel is set into motion, and lots of cogs and spikes and chains attached to humans and animals, and creatures in between, like Eduard's favourite: the monkey. The monkey is a kind of pagan god here, with a knowing face; the monkey has seen it all. The monkey in 'Self Portrait With a Monkey' hangs by the neck from a chain attached to a huge lead ball hanging in turn from the scrotum of a mechanical giant with a horned faun's head. It's their turn now. A mellow light comes on, and the seated giant begins to turn an organ grinder. He is assembled from the limbs of broken things. One of his metal legs is clad in an old army shoe. The monkey pendulum swings and the giant's foot beats in time with a Russian tune called 'Separation' that goes like this:

'Farewell, my homeland, my beloved. I will carry you with me, nothing can part us but death.'

The deep-voiced man who sings it was called Boris Axelrod, a philosopher and friend of Eduard and Tatyana's; in the 1970s he bid farewell to all he knew, courtesy of the KGB. He died in exile, on the Galilee Sea. But you have to ration your emotions here, because this is just the beginning, and you are alone in this shadow world. Tatyana and Eduard have disappeared.

Music and rattling start up behind you – another kinemat comes to life. It's 'The Castle, 1937', the most Kafkaesque work here because it is the manifestation of a recurring nightmare of Eduard's. The castle is a needle-studded torture chamber, reminiscent of the device in The Penal Colony, and one of the carved faces inside is the poet Osip Mandelstam who died in a labour camp in 1938, a year after the worst of Stalin's repressions began.

Of course Eduard's nightmare, like Kafka's, wasn't a nightmare at all – it was stark reality – up to and including the 1980s when Eduard's friend Margarita Kilmova was arrested by the KGB for disseminating books banned by the regime, and condemned to four years of prison and exile in the Soviet East. She returned terminally ill. 'The Titanic' – a dreamy contraption with wheels that turn optimistically against the current of history – is kept afloat by a stubborn little woman on the lower deck and clowns with capes and top-hats who busy themselves around the ship. They cast jagged shadows on the wall. It's dedicated to her, and it's doomed, like a silent film that you know will end very badly. Then why do you gasp with wonder?

Why are you delighted by 'Battleship of the Revolution' where a cheerful little lady skeleton with a bell on her head and red flags in her mechanical hands perches atop an old steamer, while four red oars keep turning the boat around? Round and round and round, going nowhere to the sound of a revolutionary army choir.

Why do you fall in love with the infernal romance of 'The Master and Margarita', dedicated to the memory of friend and carver Tim Stead, the man responsible for bringing the couple to Scotland? And cringe at the circus music that plays along to 'Time of Rats' where a blind mole (Russia) is abused by typewriting rats with glasses, bosoms, and important missions? And laugh nervously at 'Nikodym: the co-operation of genders' where a dumb robot gurgling with water booms nonsense in a distorted low voice (Eduard's) while the high-pitched chirping bird on his head rattles on in Tatyana's equally distorted voice? Why do you feel sick when the chained and spiked machine of 'Crusader' splutters into life? 'What a joy to march in a crowd,' – the subtitle goes – 'to be part of something, whatever the cause, whatever the banners.'

Why do you chuckle in front of the three installations grouped together as 'Proletarian Greetings', where you see the rise of Marx's 'Great Idea' to the soundtrack of a cheerful pioneers' song, then the macabre deer skull enthroned inside a cage topped with a red star and called 'The Dreamer in the Kremlin' (as H.G.Wells naively described

Lenin on a carefully edited state-tour of the USSR), and finally the melancholy 'Autumn stroll at the belle époque of Perestroika' where balloons and forgotten things from the 1980s pop out of an old suitcase, the big and small cogs keep turning, and a little accordion opens and closes like a tired lung in time with the song Moscow Nights:

> 'Everything goes quiet until dawn,
> how I love these summer Moscow nights.
> The river moves yet does not move.
> All is made from silver moon.
> A song is heard yet isn't heard
> on these quiet Moscow nights.
> I have unspoken things inside my heart.
> The river moves yet does not move.
> Don't you forget, my dear,
> these summer Moscow nights.'[1]

And why is it that, while still chuckling, you find an iceberg of sorrow melting in some forgotten place inside you?

Because you are a child in the playground of history, and you recognise injustice when you see it. Failure too. You recognise – in sound and light and music, moving coils and spikes, and slack-bellied, helplessly procreating creatures that Eduard has dreamt up for you – the truth about human endeavour. It is meaningless, but we can't give up. The dream is a nightmare, but we won't wake up from it. In Beckett's words: I can't go on, I will go on.

Because you are in an alchemical lab where shadow play, circus, and the saddest song on earth come together, you don't know how – but they do. Eduard and Tatyana make magic, and in the presence of magic you can't argue, take notes, or use big words. You can only be grateful for touching the sublime. Look, something is happening right above your head. It's a revolving two-headed poem made of skulls and horns called 'Last eagle of the Highlands' and dedicated to Mike McGrady who studied Scottish Golden eagles. Oh, and here's an industrious contraption with a cheery Highland tune. And the touching, wacky 'Rag-N-Bone Man' with John Lennon glasses and a metal bug on his ringed nose is a tribute to the traders of the shambolic Barras Market in Glasgow, where Eduard scavenges for treasures.

Tatyana sails out of the kitchen to offer you more tea. How on earth did you end up in Scotland, you ask, when you've recovered the ability to speak.

'You know, for many people from the former Soviet Union locked behind the Iron Curtain for generations, to emigrate was like to die and be born again. And some managed only the first part. We have been very lucky.'

One day in 1990, Eduard and Tatyana got a visit in their Sharmanka studio in Leningrad (St. Petersburg) from a Scottish artist couple: Tim and Maggy Stead. The visitors fell under the spell of Sharmanka, and four years later, with help from the director of Glasgow Museums Julian Spalding, organised a show in Glasgow.

Meanwhile, things in post-Soviet Russia were developing in a way that made life difficult for Eduard and Tatyana. Eduard's curse is that his creations are always, and everywhere, subversive. There is no place and no moment in history where they will stop being subversive. Post-Soviet Russia, like Soviet Russia, was not keen on subversiveness – see Mandelstam on how this is a sign of unparalleled respect – and so the couple packed up their life and emigrated to Scotland, taking Tatyana's young son Sergey with them. Circumstance ended their idyllic first few years in the Scottish countryside, and brought them to central Glasgow. They look contented with their lot.

'You know, Kapka,' Tatyana says,'It is funny. We cannot talk about politics and history with our friends here. One day, a student came from Glasgow University. He saw Sharmanka, and he was so angry. You are telling lies, he said. Stalin was great. I did not say anything.'

Eduard shuffles our way. He is bringing ginger biscuits.

'Eduard is not interested in politics,' Tatyana says.

'No, no politics,' Eduard waves irritably. 'Eat,' he puts the biscuits before me.

Of course he isn't interested in politics – he is the opposite of politics. He is a prophet, which is to say that he sees right through the fog to the heart of the matter. The heart of the matter is suffering. And suffering is brought on by illusion – this is what Eduard sees clearly, and what most of us refuse to see, for we are enamoured of our illusions.

But how do they feel about living in Socialist Realism Central, you want to know, because you carry your derangement with you.

'You have to understand, this is an industrial city,'

Tatyana says gently. 'Glasgow people were very poor. Communism is a tale for poor people. People need to believe in something.'

You can't help but notice that Tatyana and Eduard live on cabbage soup and biscuits; have never made money from Sharmanka although they've toured the world with it; just had their grant from the Scottish Arts Council cut back (strangely though, they are not in the street waving flags); and are now selling Eduard's original drawings from the 1970s. When you see these drawings, you see all of life at once, and all of the twentieth century: the tyranny of alcohol, the strangely human circus animals, the cruelty of pot-bellied bureaucracy, even a grotesque tango. As with the kinemats, you almost overlook the technical brilliance of these masterpieces because you are distracted by their terrible beauty. They plug straight into your unconscious. And they are selling for peanuts.

'No, we are not poor,' Tatyana smiles, 'On the contrary, we are rich. Because we do something we love. We have created a world that we never have to leave. We hope. Sometimes, Eduard goes to the shops to buy food. We don't even need to go out. We have here all that we need.'

It strikes you that Eduard and Tatyana are still in a state of internal emigration. That they always will be, because this is the curse, and therefore the natural state, of the true artist – to be an outsider everywhere. To inhabit the world he creates as if it is more real than the world of monuments, buildings, and placards outside. Didn't someone say that haunted places are the only ones people can live in? Eduard and Tatyana's haunted world is more real, or in any case more true.

Tatyana's son, Sergey, arrives to install new lights. He is a young man with big hands and an open face, and the youngest of the Sharmanka team. You hug Tatyana and Eduard and try not to clutch them desperately as if they are your parents.

'Dewdrop,' Eduard hugs you back, 'Come visit more often from your Edinburgh. Don't be a stranger.'

And he shuffles back to his workshop at the back, to work on a new kinemat where strange birds fly around a tree of life. Tatyana opens up the theatre for the official show at 3pm. There is a small queue outside – young people, students; some have brought sketchbooks.

The streets are dark and icy. Something has changed. You breathe more easily. You begin to see harmony in the buildings of the Merchant City. You even admire the train station, the way people are free to come and go, and nobody bats an eye-lid at the person asleep in a wheelchair, the girl with pink hair, the two kids who kiss with tongues in the sleet, the unwashed Christian with his pamphlets, the grown-up kid from Sofia with her three passports. You feel consoled by the mellow train, and the way the ticket controller smiles and calls you 'pal'.

You hear Tatyana in your head:

'In all our years here, no one ever said, What are you doing here? Never. In Russia, we have the same flowers, the same northern light and smell of the sea, the same rain. But here we also have friendly people who appreciate good craft work and the craziness of others.'

Appreciate the craziness of others – that's it. You can't believe you've been so blinded that you've missed it. Glasgow is the perfect place for the Organ Grinder to keep playing the tunes of the past and the future, and if tomorrow you moved here, the city would make space for you too, and for your derangement.

It is only in a place like this – where there is room for everything up to and including Socialist Realism, and where people are not killed for poetry – that poets like Eduard and Tatyana can live by their art.

Even if borscht is all they are having tonight.[2]

---

1. Author's translation from the Russian.

2. I am very grateful to art dealer Tony Davidson of Kilmorack Gallery who introduced me personally to Eduard and Tatyana and made this essay possible.

Brian O'Neill | *Pittsburgh*

I've often said I love Pittsburgh like a brother -- and my brother drives me nuts. The title of my book comes from a putdown I'd heard of my adopted city; "The Paris of Appalachia" is supposed to be said with a coffee-shop sneer, like "best beach in Nebraska" or "sexiest guy on 'The Benny Hill Show.'" But I see it as world-class city in a beautiful part of the world and, given enough time and enough beer, I've had little trouble making converts.

Frackin
Brian O'Neill

Pittsburgh's postcard-pretty skyline, framed by three rivers and leafy hills, offers ironic testament to how much this city has been shaped by what lies beneath us.

Take the Gulf Tower, the art-deco skyscraper with a tiered top akin to a hardened wedding cake. Though Gulf Oil is a memory here, subsumed in a 1980s merger, that 44-floor tower reminds us that Western Pennsylvania pioneered Big Oil, starting with the country's first commercial oil well and boom in Venango County in 1859.

The Gulf building was the city's tallest for nearly 40 years, until the stark, 64-floor U.S. Steel Building rose in 1970. A colossus from Day One, U.S. Steel was born when Andrew Carnegie sold his mills to JP Morgan in 1901, and for a long time it was the largest steel producer and corporation in the world. Appalachian coal fed its massive riverside factories and the Allegheny, Monongahela and Ohio rivers were the highways for its product and supply.

Today, all steel mills are gone from Pittsburgh proper and not only has U.S. Steel sold its namesake tower, it's no longer even the tenant with top billing. UPMC, the global health conglomerate and modern engine of the regional economy, has the top five floors and its name slapped across the top.

Yet it's still called the U.S. Steel Tower, reminding us that Pittsburgh is where it is, and is what it is, largely because of geologic phenomena going back hundreds of millions of years. In our fast-forward world, a new extraction boom is likely to change Pittsburgh yet again.

It was only August 2007 that Range Resources hit natural gas gushers in Washington County, south of Pittsburgh. The state recorded 76 wells drilled into the "Marcellus Shale" that year. By the start of 2012, nearly 3,000 had been drilled. This sedimentary rock beneath the Appalachian range has become synonymous with natural gas drilling the likes of which the eastern United States hasn't seen in a hundred years.

International investment has been staggering. Royal Dutch Shell paid $4.7 billion in 2010 for a suburban Pittsburgh leasing company; Chevron paid $4.3 billion in 2011 for a rival stake; Exxon Mobil followed with a $1.69 billion buy for two more local drillers.

These multinationals are merely the biggest names. The Pennsylvania Department of Environmental Protection literally hasn't been able to keep up. The Pittsburgh Post-Gazette discovered early in 2012 that the DEP had listed 495 more wells producing gas, or ready to produce gas, than it ever had recorded being drilled.

The gas bonanza has meant work for many blue-collar men, a group that had been pummeled in this region and across America as manufacturing jobs disappeared. Due at least in part to the gas boom, the unemployment rate in Pittsburgh's seven-county metro area has stayed well below state and national numbers for years now.

The sudden spike in supply has made gas considerably cheaper, too; it hit its lowest price in a decade in 2012, which caused some companies to announce cutbacks in their Marcellus plays. Electrical costs are also shrinking as coal-fired electrical plants are switching to cleaner burning natural gas. As if that weren't enough, President Barack Obama touted natural gas in his 2012 State of the Union message as a way for America to slash its dependence on foreign oil. Industrialists need only come up with more natural gas-powered vehicles and, some suggest, electric-motored cars will be stalled yet again.

So why does all this drilling scare the daylights out of so many? Because the process is so new and freakish or, more to the point, "frackish." Instead of drilling straight down, the modus operandi in the Marcellus Shale is called "fracking." Drillers descend straight down at first, but then go diagonally, and finally horizontally within the shale formation a mile or more down, greatly extending the reach. After setting off explosions to fracture the shale, millions of gallons of chemically treated water (most of which is gone from the land surface forever) and sand is pumped in at high pressure. The freed gas is captured by pipe and carried to the surface.

Its proponents argue that the impact is well below the water table and would have to make the impossible climb through layers of rock and against gravity to reach the aquifer. Its many detractors remind us that a break in the pipe can lead to gas migration and contamination of the drinking water. That's already happen, and critics also suggest the process is so new we can't know exactly where the gas, or the treated water, might travel over time.

We're talking about gas but the situation is fluid. With the ultimate impact unknown, we're sure only that the industry is throwing a lot of money around. Some of it employs people and buys American manufacturing, and some of it goes into campaign coffers and may buy politicians.

Thus far both the Republican-controlled state Legislature and Republican Governor Tom Corbett have been very accommodating. Pennsylvania has remained the only big gas-drilling state with no severance tax. Though the leading industry group has said repeatedly it could accept such a tax (it's part of the cost of doing business everywhere else], Gov. Corbett seems keen to out-Texas Texas.

A battle is now playing out between local governments and the state government.

The industry's Marcellus Shale Coalition, citing its shrinking profit margins, seeks statewide uniformity in drilling rules to ease production costs, but local governments bristle over losing control over such a high-impact industry. Local impact fees have been stalled by legislative squabbles, even as trucks with Texas and Oklahoma plates fill formerly quiet two-lane Pennsylvania roads 24/7.

There need be no rush to get all this right. It's not like we're talking about green bananas here, and proximity to Northeast markets means Pennsylvania gas won't ever have the transportation costs that southern and western fossil fuels do. But there's always a rush when there are billions of dollars to be made.

Gov. Corbett says this gas "will power our state's economic engine for generations to come" and "give our children a reason to stay in Pennsylvania." As he pushed for increased distance of well setbacks from private wells and public water systems, and increased fees for bonding against drillings mishaps, Mr. Corbett promised, "We are going to do this safely and we're going to do it right, because energy equals jobs."

Critics worry there are jobs in disaster relief, too.

For many in the city and inner suburbs, all they know of these (often literally) earth-shaking changes is what they read in the newspapers, see on TV or hear on the radio. The drilling is all around Allegheny County but rarely in it, and then only in the sparsely populated outer edge. Pittsburgh City Council banned gas drilling in November 2010, a move that was largely symbolic because the city's density and distance from any pipeline makes drilling there an unnecessary headache given all the other options.

But that epitomized the concern. Then City Councilman Doug Shields cited Article 1, Section 27 of the Pennsylvania Constitution as he made his case for the strongest anti-drilling law:

"The people have the right to clean air, pure water, and to the preservation of the natural, scenic, historic and esthetic values of the environment. Pennsylvania's public natural resources are the common property of all the people, including generations yet to come. As trustee of these resources, the Commonwealth shall conserve and maintain them for the benefit of all the people."

Many don't trust that the state to play that role,

though, hence the clamor from township, borough and city councils for more local control.

We are living in relatively good times in Pittsburgh. We didn't suffer the real estate implosion so much of the country did because we never sent home prices spiking in the first place. But our history reminds us that it's difficult to predict the course of fossil-fuel based industries even a decade ahead, much less generations.

Don Carter, director of the Remaking Cities Institute at the CMU School of Architecture, has argued in recent years that we need to quit calling Pittsburgh and the rest of the industrial Midwest "the Rust Belt" and start calling it "the Water Belt." The Sun Belt can be called the Drought Belt, Mr. Carter says.

The two most vital resources – energy and water – are in abundance here.

In short, Marcellus Shale drilling can be the best thing to happen to Western Pennsylvania if we can get to it without destroying Western Pennsylvania. That may be overstating both ends of the equation, but it is as the rival camps see it.

American Sonnet for Wanda C.
Terrance Hayes

Who I know knows why all those lush boned worn out girls are
Whooping at where the moon should be, an eyelid clamped
On its lightness. Nobody sees her without the hoops firing in her
Ears because nobody sees. Tattooed on her forearms she claims
Is BRING ME TO WHERE MY BLOOD RUNS and I want that to be here
Where I am her son, pent in blackness and turning the night's calm
Loose and letting the same fires run through me. In her bomb hair:
Shells full of thunder, in her mouth the fingers of some calamity,
Somebody foolish enough to love her foolishly. Those who could hear
No music weren't listening—and when I say it, it's like claiming
She's an elegy. It rhymes, because of her, with effigy. Because of her
If there is no smoke there is no party. I think of you Miss Calamity
Every Sunday. I think of you on Monday. I think of you hurling hurt
where the moon should be and stomping into our darkness calmly.

Will Self | *Glasgow*

On 'relationship': Self has a long association with Scotland. He lived in the Orkney Islands in the early 1990s and for ten years regularly went there to write. He's married to the journalist Deborah Orr, a native of Motherwell, and they spend a lot of time walking up and down the banks of the Clyde and wondering whether or not just press on the next 15-odd miles into Glasgow. Of the city itself Self recently wrote in a review piece about Owen Hatherley's 'The New Ruins of Britain', apropos of the notorious Red Road development: The burnt-out playground and other derelict facilities that stud the lumpy forecourts of the blocks could not, in my estimation, ever have compensated for the wilful inappositeness of these structures that were funnelling down the icy northerlies: there's always been enough brutality in Glasgow to go round, so Brutalism seems excessive.'

Night Walk
Will Self

Joachim Schlör in his seminal study 'Nights in the Big City', writes how the coming of street lighting, to Western cities in the mid-19th century, was attended by an upsurge in moral panic. Far from experiencing the illumination as the banishment of infernal darkness, many burghers perceived a dangerous and unnatural phenomenon. The lit-up city was a realm within which the established divisions between interior and exterior were broken down: no longer did the good citizen lock up his door at nightfall, and wait for the cock's crow.

By the same token, street lighting allowed for the mingling of classes and sexes in new and promiscuous ways – so nightlife was born. The ability to move easily about the city, traversing zones heretofore off-limits and penetrating sequestered neighbourhoods, crystallised urban self-consciousness. The city dwellers were now permanently checking themselves in the lit windows of shops, and seeing there, imprisoned, Escher-like, their own reflection and the images of that which they desired.

Even in our own era, a hundred and forty years later, the city by night still appears as a distinctively modern terrain: at once minatory and compelling, too bright and too obscure. The shadows are sharply adumbrated, the colours are leeched out, the people stroll, hurry and lurk, players on a stage set that has been erected For One Night Only.

Any serious flaneur walks by night as much as by day; for by day it's too easy to be drawn into a complacent acceptance of normalcy. This much we plainly know: the panel truck disgorging toilet paper; the smoking secretary with laddered tights; the dosser senatorial, sporting a sleeping bag for a toga. But by night these are shapeshifters, capable of defeating our expectations. They may assume the faces of loved ones, and so effortlessly enforce intimacy – or seem strange to point of being alien, and so provoke repulsion. We may fancy ourselves rational and civilised, yet immediately beyond the sodium firelight, the wolves are always pacing the paving stones.

I walk by night. I remember years ago, before there were buses or tubes on New Year's Eve, walking over London Bridge, in the chill of the first 3.00 a.m. of the year, and seeing an entire platoon of Roman Legionnaires come marching towards me. At the front a standard bearer carried the Eagle captioned 'SPQR', at the back a drummer in a leopard skin beat the rhythm for their sandaled feet.

I was not alone, so could not dismiss this as fancy or hallucination. Yet, neither my companions nor I, were disposed to talk to each other as the ancient squad passed us by; nor did we hail them, nor did we speak of it again. It was a benison of the night.

I have trudged through the dust of Varanasi in Uttar Pradesh, by the 40 watt-lighted sheds, where everything mechanical that can be dismantled is bolted together again; and by the candle-guttering hovels, where women knead chapatti dough as dun as the walls of their own, malleable dwellings.

In the heat of the night cities exhale: ghee sizzles and releases the food smells into the dark, where human minds, starved of vision, open up their nostrils to see. By night all hot cities are synaesthetic, in this way: scrambling up sound and smell and touch, so that a milk train, clacking over points, feels up your spine with metallic fingertips.

I have walked uptown from the Village, on Halloween night, passing by the raggedy company of ghoulish New Yorkers, all Gothed-up in Gotham, their eyes black-rimmed, their teeth bloodstained. We were carrying our eldest son, then a newborn baby, and Morticia after Cruella stopped to bill and coo: 'Is that a real baby?'

Is this a real city? was the only possible rejoinder. In the chill darkness New York forfeits any claim on our amazement. The pinprick lights of the vertiginous towers merge with the empyrean itself, while at ground level, fire hydrant after phone booth after Korean corner shop provide the delusions of human scale. It's all about us, isn't it? Along the long ramps of the avenue, taxis wallow, their grimacing fenders gulp up the devilish steam clouds escaping from manholes, then their trunks release them in vaporous gouts.

But tonight I'm not in the east or the south or the west, not in Varanasi or London or New York, I'm in Glasgow, dining with the writer Alasdair Gray and his wife, Morag. I'm not thinking about night walking especially. We're sitting in the brasserie of the Óran Mor, the arts centre on the corner of Byres Road and the Great Western. Upstairs, on the ceiling of the enormous nave – it was once a Presbyterian church with a pituitary disorder – Alasdair has painted one of his distinctive murals: Zodiacal figures striking hieratic attitudes against the vaulted blue sky.

There is the deep blue of the night sky in his mural, and Alasdair and his co-workers have scattered silvery stars across it. Of course, the anti-naturalism of this is all the more poignant in the heart of the city, where the constant haemorrhaging of electric light bleeds sodium into the darkness. We use different parts of the eye – rods and cones – with which to see colour; at night, in the absence of electric light, we see the world in a ghostly monochrome; or rather, we see it in a beautiful, silver nitrate monochrome, if only we allow it to swim out of the dark fluid for us: night sight takes time to develop – at least a half hour. Instead of this ulterior vision, the city the splashes Day-Glo red, blue and orange across our eyes, and it's only in their lurid afterimages that we become creepily aware: the silhouette of the beast remains in the shadows.

Alasdair is speaking of Flann O'Brien and a conceit that he particularly likes in 'The Third Policeman': 'You recall,' he squeak-says, in his distinctively staccato manner, alternating between parody and self-parody, 'the character of, um, de Selby, and his, ah, theory that night, far from being darkness, is, in fact, a morbid exhalation of some kind: "black air". De Selby didn't know that much about the, um, black air, although he had reached the conclusion – following certain ex-per-i-ments, that it must be a gas – because when he lit a candle, it burned, and the black air, ah, dissipated!'

Alasdair's words inspire me, and I decide to walk

back to my hotel, the Hilton at Charing Cross. I like to stay at the Hilton when I'm in Glasgow, a tower block of faux-domesticity by the M8 flyover, from its prow-shaped windows it offers the biggest views out over the valley of the Clyde, or out towards its mouth, or north, into the hills at Mingavie. I can't sleep well in hotels: sleep is too big a descent into the black air with nothing familiar around you. The French have it wrong, it isn't orgasm that's the 'little death', but sleep – even an afternoon nap in a hotel is a micro-extinction for me. In the severe rationality of the Hilton's shoebox rooms, the owlish visitor, alone and sick of the TV lightbox, can turn his attention outwards, and imagine himself flying up into the sky, buffeted by grey Zeppelins of cloud, their undersides bilious from the street lighting.

India, seen by night from high above, is a diadem of a subcontinent, jewelled by the faint gleam of its myriad villages scattered regularly across the Gangetic plain. The lambency of the earth's cities is visible from space: a Cosmonaut, or an American billionaire, who steps out from the Mir space station for a short walk, must find himself stroll-orbiting on this pavement of lights. A 20,000 mph constitutional from the few remaining dark patches of the world – its increasingly tepid poles, and equatorial bald spots – to the mighty blaze of Western Europe, the east and western seaboards of North America, where untold ergs of energy are hurled skyward: Zeus's thunderbolts returned to him with a vengeance.

I say goodbye to Alasdair and Morag and leave. Suddenly, I'm standing outside the brasserie looking at man with a fighter-pilot moustache, who's leaning, smoking, against a steel bollard. It's a chilly night in the north, and we've been forced to acquire the habit of exile, along with our other one. The transition from interior to exterior is that much more extreme by night. Thrust into the chill and unsettling city, what could be more understandable than the newly primitive desire to light a small fire and warm your lips round it?

He stares balefully over at me, his fighter must look like an enormous cigarette – so nictoninous is his facial hair.

'Why've they put 'em there?' He grunts, jerking a thumb at some metal tables and chairs outside the adjoining pub.

'I imagine they're looking forward to the summer.' I say. He grinds out his butt and comes up to impress his walrus muzzle on me:

'Oh, aye,' he groans, 'mebbe.'

'It's the triumph,' I say, sententiously, 'of hope over expectation.'

This pricks his interest and he peers at me with watery-eyed gratitude. Looking at his saggy denim arse as he shuffles back into the pub, it occurs to me that this may be the first time in weeks that anyone has addressed him as if he possesses a brain not sodden.

I set off to walk the two or three miles back to my hotel. It's that paradoxical time of year, poised on the cusp of spring, when some urbanites huddle up while others strip off. To some, the night is a velvet cloak to be draped around their bare shoulders, to others it's black ice insinu-

ated between stubbly neck and furry collar. By a post office box a waif stands with her chapped lips riveted together, and the bright pink stippling of goose bumps on
her white, white calves.

I think of long evenings when summer is finally here.
In London, where I live, there are no Dosteovskian 'white
nights', such as you get here in the north; instead, the
heat seems to build into the dusk, a mounting rhythm as
all the exhaust fumes, rubber, leather and grease pounded
into the paving stones and tarmac reaches a critical mass,
before exhaling into the cooling air. At those times, walking back from the West End, seeing the strollers on the
Embankment in shorts and T-shirts, or the clones outside
the Vauxhall Tavern, shaven-headed and bare-chested, the
night time city is a boudoir, with its sexed-up inhabitants
in increasing states of deshabille.

I head away from the main road, up glistening pavements between privet hedges. There's the faintest of miz-
zles, a percolation of water into the air, so that in the
down light of the streetlamps sparkly, diaphanous curtains
waver and distort. The houses are large and handsome;
their porticos are rendered in stone and supported by Gre-
cian pillars. Urns and petrified laurel wreaths are poised
on head-height gateposts. Through the clear panes of one
sash window I see a couple, a wine bottle, incendiary
news footage on a television by the fireplace. I cover their
framed art exhibition posters, their tufted rug, their family
photos more than anything I've ever wanted before. Nothing and nobody is more covetable than a cosy dwelling,
seen by night from the street without. The sash window

is a shop window and what's for sale here is an idea of cosy homeliness that can never be experienced, except by a voyeur.

On I plod, past the unutterable gloom of a silent, suburban church, down an alleyway and back on to the main road. The parked cars are now pearlised with raindrops; a take-out chef kneels to close his shop grille with a rattle; the enlarged photos in the furniture store are portraits of the ideal, - yet absent – family that lives here. There are also pubs and shops along this paving stone strand, young people stand out in the street, smoking and drinking from clear bottles full some fluid rendered bilious by the sodium glare of the streetlamps. I'm entering their territory, and everything in their body language – the way they butt and rut, the way they preen and keen – suggests that they guard it zealously. Yet, I'm invisible, beneath my own magical cloak of middle age. By day strangers can be scrutinised, by night we are reduced to the crudest approximations: age, gender, height, bulk, and dismissed accordingly.

Turning down another quiet street - this time one lined by the flat facades of two-up, two-down terraced houses – I'm discomfited by the presence of a fellow night walker; a woman, trim and well-dressed, who clacks along the pavement on high heals. I feel that dreadful sense of reverse paranoia that always comes upon me when I find myself walking behind a single woman by night; and this time, as I am in a melancholy mood, it's intensified. Night walking is a luxury for a man such as myself, too old to attract casual aggro, too large to be easy prey. It's worth remembering that for many others the night time city is

a genuine jungle, not merely a psychic adventure playground.

At the next corner the orange wash of artificial light
and the brown miasma of the shadows, is slashed apart by
the revolving blue blades that coruscate from the roof of a
police car. Two officers stand either side of a rubbish bag
full of humanity that's draped over a garden wall. Their
fluorescent jackets give them the appearance of plastic
bafflers arranged around a traffic accident. The cheap jew-
ellery of broken glass lies scattered on the pavement at
their feet.

I'm relieved by the presence of the police – it damps
down my reverse paranoia. The woman ahead of us fum-
bles in her handbag for her key, and opens the front door
of the house next door. I pass by, ignored by all. Come
dawn, all that will be left of this incident are the contents
of an abused stomach fertilising an herbaceous border.
Oh! Those herbaceous borders, those privet hedges floc-
culent and strong-smelling by night, more bucolic than
any country lane.

Then, a grand building, A huge, elongated dome,
two L-shaped wings bracket a courtyard, and flap away
the night. It takes me what seem like aeons to proceed
along its frontage, beside its punitive iron railings, under
the stare of its hundreds of blank windows. Then, quite
suddenly, we can see the city spread out below and to our
right, a sparking grid of streets; while ahead, the motorway
flyover strides on blocky concrete legs, its deck swishing
with speedy, late-night traffic.

By night, the underside of the flyover is a cloistral

space – but writ unbelievably large. I decide to work my way down the slip road, past behemoth Indian restaurants, and go underneath it on to a patch of wasteland. This - it occurs to me, as I struggle over mounds of shattered masonry and through inappropriate thistle patches – is the real temple of modernity. This is the city's Baalbec, with its bulbous pillars, its Byzantine illuminations, its altar of traffic lights. I remember being in San Francisco, a few months after the earthquake, and walking by night beside a flyover such as this, but one buckled and broken. It felt like a total reversal of civilisation, a halting progress back to the primeval.

A scamper across the slip road, a traverse across a car park, up a ramp, and there it is: the bland uniformity of the hotel, rising up twenty storeys, each lighted window another desperate little tale. The electric doors whoosh open and I'm yanked into the lobby. Even though I've only been walking for an hour, it's enough to completely destabilise me. In here, everything is too close up, too in yer-face, too large and bright and insistent. Shaven-headed businessman bouncers stand on a quarter-acre of carpet, giving each other strong-arm handshakes, breaking into one another's personality.

Our ancestors were right it seems, to fear the lighting of the city; for, by banishing the night from the outside, we've sucked it into our own interiors.

Gerry Stern | *Pittsburgh*

I have a love-hate relationship with Pittsburgh. I hate the violence, ethnic hatred, entitlement of the rich, filth, and lying of my early years in Pittsburgh, but I equally dislike, to a certain degree, the disappearance of Pittsburgh as a vital industrial city. All of which doesn't make sense. I loved--and love--the hills, the secret valleys, the tunnels, the bridges, the ethnic neighborhoods, the crowded downtown (especially of my memory), the place--source--hope--of my own development. It wasn't easy being a first-generation Jew in those days, nor was it easy being Polish, Black and the rest. I learned most of all to resist the oppression, latent or explicit, of the powerful.

The Frick Mansion
Gerry Stern

Figuring up what you might call an exchange,
and only for a painting but not counting
the claim of a share in the sixty rooms or counting
a share of the inflation compared to the mean
reduction of so many bodies in such a heavy
cardboard box or two, I'd say three hundred
fifty to seven hundred fifty, taking in
a complicated system of matching death payments
with the cost of buying or stealing, or I'd say
three hundred dead Slovaks for one Caravaggio.

Died in the Mills

Then, fifty dollars for a Hungarian
say a black dress to go to the funeral
and shoes with soles for the three oldest, that leaves
a dollar fifty for the feast but I'd say
what a dollar was worth then you could have
a necktie if you wanted and paprikash
for twenty or thirty and strudel with apples and nuts
and violins—he favored the violin—
and it is not just poets that love meadows
and take their sneakers off and their socks to walk
on the warm rocks and dip their tender white feet
in the burning freezing water and then bend down
precariously to pick up a froglet and sight
the farthest lonely tree and note the wind
moving quickly through the grasses their last summer.

The Train Station

Throughout history men and women have found a certain peace in that strange place we call sky. It was, and is, the source of vision, memory, hope, ideals, and even historical connections. All we know is there in the sky. Not in the planets, the stars, the formations—I love that too, but I think mostly of sky—a daytime sky—with clouds and sun and water—and the colors. It is the upper regions of the air, it is the heavens, the celestial region. Heaven itself, the foolish place. And sometimes the entire sky every which way you look is covered with clouds, from the ground up, it seems, as if it were a tent of white, a Mongolian tent, enormous and round and here and there a hole, a blue hole, in the fabric so the blue dust can get in or so we can see out, oh here and there into the great expanse, what they call firmament. Though sometimes, in a great cave, in a cathedral, in a huge train station, there is a simulacrum of this sky and once in the silence of the main hall of the Pennsylvania Railroad, in Pittsburgh, ten or eleven at night, I was caught in the endless space. The roof was so distant it was almost invisible. And there was nothing there but three wagons, one broken, two waiting to be pulled. For a second I was alone. We had not yet loaded the wagons and attached ourselves like mules, pulling the boxes and loading the freight cars for our eight hours, from five p.m. to one in the morning, the smell of sulfur our drug. There was no happiness like that. There was only obedience to the heft, and if our heads were often bent forward to assist our shoulders and arms, it was the slight wind and the hard rubber on the concrete and the mysterious cog in the heart of the wagon that helped us. Though sometimes we were aided by the leftover straw from a previous load, and sometimes we swore we were going downhill. There was no motor and no pneumatic inflated tires. If there was deep attention, there was no divine assistance; and sometimes there were two of us, and sometimes one, and sometimes we were overtaken by the weight of things and our forward momentum. If there was grace we hardly knew it and if there was joy it was when the first box—or carton—was lifted up over the steel rim; it was when the wagon ceased to be that huge and menacing—and we found nothing lurking there invisible to our touch. And the weight of the boxes increasing as we reached bottom. The return so fast we ran.

Mitch Miller | *Glasgow*

GLASGOW DIALECTOGRAMS

Mitch Miller

Pages 120-121 of this book contains a section of a 'dialectogram' of one of the 50 or so Showman's Yards found in Glasgow. The 6,000 people who live in this city within a city, tucked into Glasgow's quietest and hardest to find corners, represent about 80% of the Travelling Show-people whose traditional routes of fairs, galas and high days cover Scotland and the northern England. Glasgow is home to the highest concentration of travelling entertainer communities Europe, my own family is among them. The drawing here is very similar to the yard they occupy – the one I think of as 'home', that place where a small crumb of your childhood remains intact – this is a grown man's drawing of home.

Travelling showpeople are a gregarious, good humoured and easy going bunch, but they are also very private people. An earlier version of this drawing I produced in 2009 had full 'documentary' value – it named names and went into minute detail, with the result that I was asked, very nicely, to withdraw it from public view, though it was made clear that all of the families from the original would be happy to see themselves appear in a drawing under a different name. In this redrawn, updated version none of the names here (the Kelsos, Francises, Marshalls and so forth) relate to showground families you will actually find in Scotland, but each name has a carnival 'ring' to it. Those with an existing knowledge of the community will be able to work out exactly who Robert Kelso and Janie Marcel really are, but those without such knowledge can be assured that with the exception of the names, the information is 'real' enough.

So much for the subjects - the reader may be more perplexed at exactly what a 'dialectogram' is. The straightest answer I can give is that they are big documentary drawings (about 47 inches x 34 inches, or the top of a good sized coffee table) of places I have frequented in Glasgow. The most honest answer is that they are a weak joke gone too far. I coined the term to describe that first drawings of showman's yard, a diagram that contained subjective information, vernacular speech and terminology and a hand-drawn aesthetic (dialect or dialectic + diagram = dialectogram. Hilarious, isn't it?).

Instead of rolling their eyes as they should have, peers and people with commissioning budgets started lodging suggestions for other parts of Glasgow that I could draw. On my books at the moment are the Red Road flats, an archaeological dig in Queens Park and a pub in the south side (the last of these involving very strenuous research at the bar). Worse than that, people began to use the term 'dialectogram' as if it were a proper word! The point is of course, that there is nothing proper about it, although it is perhaps appropriate that a word I made up as I went along describes these glimpses of an ad hoc city; I like to draw its transient, hidden, threatened often vulnerable edges, those districts where an old steel foundry hides a hamlet of side-show folk, its old rusted gate a portal to an honest-to-God, parallel universe that has been dancing cheek to cheek with yours for over 150 years.

The full version of this and other Glasgow Dialectograms can be viewed at www.dialectograms.co.uk

Charlee Brodsky | *Pittsburgh*

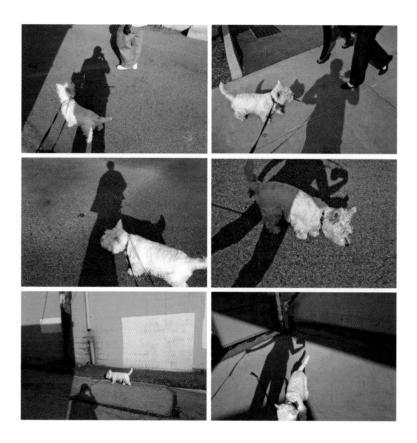

Charlee Brodsky

from *Max the Dog*

Doug Cooper

October - Game Night

July - Summer Evening on Diulus

Mitch Miller

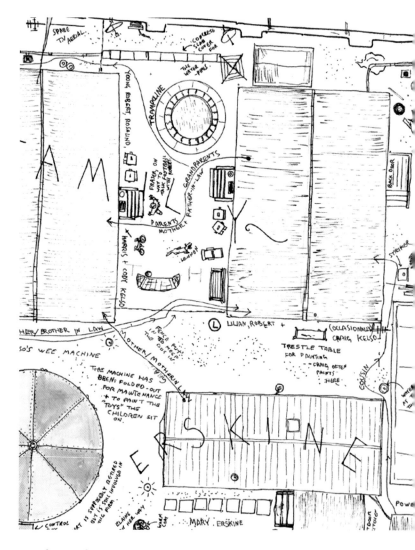

from *Showman's Yard Dialectogram*

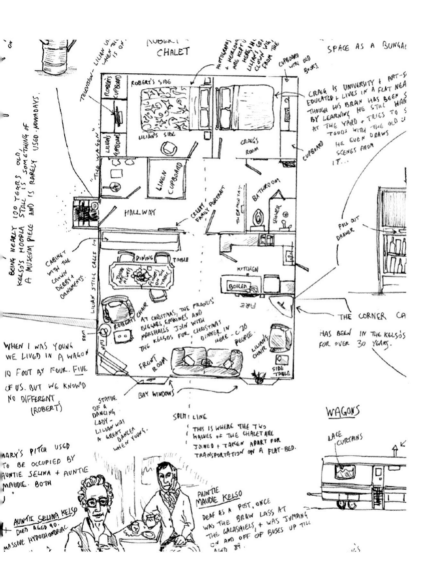

ROBERT'S CHALET

SPACE AS A BUNGAL...

PHOTOGRAPHY - WILLIAN MRS KEPT US
AND MRS HUSSEIN LILIAN'S CLOUDIES WHEN
THE VAN THE

ROBERT'S SIDE

ROBERT'S CUPBOARD

LILIAN'S CUPBOARD

"THE WAGON"

LILIAN'S SIDE

CUPBOARD WITH OLD BOOKS

CRAIG IS UNIVERSITY + ART-S...
EDUCATED + LIVES IN A FLAT NEA...
THOUGH HIS BRAIN HAS BEEN S...
BY LEARNING HE STILL HAR...
AT THE YARD + TRIES TO S...
TOUGH WITH THE OLD ...
HE EVEN DRAWS
SCENES FROM
IT...

CRAIG'S ROOM

CUPBOARD

BATHROOM

SHOWER

LINEN CUPBOARD

HALLWAY

CREEPY FAMILY PORTRAIT

THE MAGIC TAP

PULL OUT DRAWER

CABINET WITH THE CHINA DERBY + ORNAMENTS

DINING TABLE

KITCHEN

BOILER

FIRE

THE CORNER CA...

HAS BEEN IN THE KELSO'S
FOR OVER 30 YEARS.

ROBERT'S CHAIR

AT CHRISTMAS, THE FRANCIS'
BIGGARS, EHRNES AND
MARSHALLS JOIN WITH
THE KELSOS FOR CHRISTMAS
DINNER IN HERE - c 20
PEOPLE

LILIAN'S CHAIR

SIDE TABLE

FRONT ROOM

BAY WINDOWS

Being nearly 100 years old,
Kelso's Moobla
Stall is something of
a museum piece and is rarely used nowadays.

LILIAN STILL CALLS IT

FROM

WHEN I WAS YOUNG
WE LIVED IN A WAGON
10 FOOT BY FOUR. FIVE
OF US. BUT WE KNOWED
NO DIFFERENT
(ROBERT)

STATUE OF A DANCING LADY -
LILIAN WAS A GREAT DANCER
WHEN YOUNG.

SPLIT LINE
THIS IS WHERE THE TWO
HALVES OF THE CHALET ARE
JOINED + TAKEN APART FOR
TRANSPORTATION ON A FLAT-BED.

WAGONS

LACE CURTAINS

MARY'S PITCH USED
TO BE OCCUPIED BY
AUNTIE SELINA + AUNTIE
MAUDIE. BOTH

AUNTIE SELINA KELSO
DIED AGED 90.
MASSIVE HYPOCHONDRIAC

AUNTIE MAUDIE KELSO
DEAF AS A POST, ONCE
WAS THE BRAW LASS AT
THE GALASHIELS, + WAS JUMPING
ON AND OFF OF BUSES UP TILL
AGED 89.

- 121 -

Gordon Burnistoun

Glasgow image 01

Glasgow image 02

Peter Mackie Burns

stills from *Come Closer*

Peter Mackie Burns | *Glasgow*

Dear Mr Billy Connolly

You don't know me as I am relatively speaking a nobody whereas you are Billy Connolly uber Comedian and much under rated but award winning actor etc but you already know that!

As a much loved son of this fair city I hope you also know how highly held in esteem and affection you are in Glasgow and around the globe! Including Canada, America, Parts of the New World etc etc. Personally, I must say in all the years I have listened to you or watched your videos films telly even cassettes dvds and blu rays records etc you have always come across as a thoroughly decent human being and are still funny as fuck although you haven't lived here for years. That isn't a criticism just an observation. I've heard you get back here quite a bit though and I admire that about you.You are still approachable and a real person. Plus you need to keep finding new material, i would imagine, and see new things and places and meet new folk and all that before you die (Hope that never happens). This brings me to my point. In a pub called Otto on Byres Road (Formerly called The Rubyiat. You might remember it from years ago when you had your widely documented struggle with alcohol issues?) Well in the gents toilets there is a CD of yours playing constantly on a loop. Everytime you go in to spend a penny or what have you your voice is there telling stories and it is terrific. Seriously. Folk actually stop what they are doing to just listen. I don't know if they have it in the ladies toilets but if they don't then they should. It is a nice wee surprise when it happens, especially the first time, and stops urinating etc being just run of the mill. I've actually stayed in the toilet much longer than i have really needed to on a few occasions to listen to the end of one of your jokes. Everybody talks it about when they sit back down at their tables. They play it constantly in Otto's toliet day and night i believe and have done for a year or maybe longer. Its kind of like a living memorial if that isn't too disgusting a thing to say? Much Better than a statue and more practical. Next time your back in Glasgow if you ever need a pish pop in and try it. Imagine blokes faces in there if they are doing a pee and you open the cubicle door and come out. Classic! Never know I might see you there! (Joke!!!!) All the best Billy. We love you.

Yours faithfully
Peter Mackie 0141 555 7462

Doug Cooper | *Pittsburgh*

I was not born in Pittsburgh. During most of my child-hood, my family lived in Connecticut. But in August 1953, when I was six, I decided my true home was Pittsburgh.

It was the year after my grandfather had died of can-cer. My father often came to Pittsburgh on business, and he took me with him, on the night train, to visit my grand-mother.

I lay awake most of the night watching the world pass by the lower berth window. My first views of Pitts-burgh were of its periphery and, in half-light, the Horse-shoe Curve, steam trains pulling coal cars out of the night: views with reflected moons and clouds down over the Connemaugh River leading to the mills at Johnstown. It was an incremental sense of the city, not the sudden intro-duction one gets today arriving by plane. It was as if the elements that made up Pittsburgh's approaching chemistry were laid out for inspection, one by one in sequence: first the hills, then the coal, then the valleys, then the water, and finally the fire.

We passed under the Westinghouse Bridge when we were in the dining car. Below us and alongside Westing-house Airbrake, Turtle Creek flowed a color yellow I had never seen before.

"There's a story about this bridge." All of a sudden

my father spoke over his coffee. "When they were pour-
ing the concrete, one of the workers fell into the form.
You can't get them out during a pour. They leave them
in. He's still in there." I imagined him still in there, still
drowning in the concrete, still trying to swim to the top of
the pour.

Then the valley widened, and while the train round-
ed the bend overlooking Braddock, the smoke and fire
plumes of the Edgar Thomson steel works rose beside us.
It was a layered scene, rust brown haze and red heat in
the foreground with dark stacked profiles behind. Peek-
a-boo morning light reflected past the sheds and furnaces
from the distant Monongahela River. Gas jets fired overhead. Then, just as quickly, the view closed again as the
train turned into the cut through Swissvale. House-house-
house-house-house-street,   house-house-house-house-
house-street, the rhythm gained speed on the long straight-
away through Wilkinsburg but could not dull my sense of
awe for this fire-land where people were buried drowning
in concrete....

Pittsburgh, as it was during my week with my grandmother, and Pittsburgh, as it still was when I later went to Carnegie Tech, still burns at the center of my memory, still
draws me to its shadow and light. Though the land has
been savaged, it has been good for me to live near the fire
where things have been made. I still see the poured slag
rolling down the valleys and lighting the rows of houses
and the hillsides in reflected afterglow. As in the pulse of
summer lightning, the houses and the land seem to have

but two natures; either they are shadow and material or they are light.

Scientists write that in the beginning there was light and that the material of the universe and the earth itself cooled out of the primal bang. Material is congealed light. Material and light are paired opposites; the one came from the other.

For years now I have drawn Pittsburgh in charcoal murals. Charcoal is burned wood. It is fire that was. I use the charcoal for the shadows. I use the white of the paper for the light. And it has been this one moment between shadow and light that thrills me; as the Bessemer is turned, as the slag is poured, as the furnace is tapped, when the shadow and light flare out, the world watches transfixed by the transforming fire.

Doug Johnstone | *Glasgow*

I'm an outsider in Glasgow, an interloper. I've never lived there, and it has such a different atmosphere to the east coast of Scotland where I grew up, and to Edinburgh where I now live. Sometimes I feel like I should get my passport stamped at Queen Street Station when I go through. But I like that outsider feeling, it allows me to observe the place and the people from a detached distance. I think some of that dislocation has bled into the main character in my story. I hope so, anyway.

I'm Yours to Knock Around
Doug Johnstone

He closed his eyes and tried to block out the sound of Glasgow. He opened his eyes. The pub was rammed, blasted with voices, too bright. He was squeezed into a corner next to the slate fireplace, building up a sweat and gripping his pint.

Connie was at the toilet. He looked around Babbity's. The barmaids were the only women he could see. Gangs of middle-aged men clamoured for attention at the bar, racing to get a final pint of cooking or wife-beater before they bolted along the road to Celtic Park.

If Nick had realised there was an Old Firm game tonight, he wouldn't have suggested going out. Couldn't be doing with this. The pub was full of accents, salt of the earth bullshit. But it was harmless enough, this was a middle class place after all. He dreaded to think of the pubs nearer the ground.

He followed the football, but not the Old Firm. He was a lower league fan, real football. Arbroath, where he'd been brought up, before his folks moved to Dundee.

He came to Glasgow for love. Followed Connie. He hated it here, but it was home now.

Connie squeezed her way between stocky, white-haired men in overcoats. They were old but they still checked out her tits and arse in a way that made sure she noticed.

Nick noticed too. He imagined cracking his pint glass off the table and lifting it into the nearest guy's face. That would get some respect.

Connie looked tired, beautiful but tired.

She lifted her eyebrows as if to say, 'We picked a night for it, eh?'

'Cheers,' he said, tapping his pint against hers. 'Happy anniversary.'

'Happy anniversary.'

A dry kiss, then they both drank.

'I shouldn't have pints,' she said. 'I can't handle it anymore. I'll be hammered after two.'

Three years since Danny was born, that was all, but they'd gone from drug-gobbling all-nighters to barely being able to share a glass of wine without falling asleep on the sofa. Tonight was a waste of money they didn't have. But he'd suggested it to try and reignite something.

Danny hadn't been diagnosed, but he wasn't right. ADHD or OCD, or maybe just a fucking tantrum merchant. They'd taken him to doctors but never got anywhere, despite Connie's contacts. Just high spirits, one of them said. If only he could see the boy at his worst.

And Nick had to deal with it all, he was the one at home. He couldn't complain, Connie earned the wage, paid the bills, gave him money for traumatic shopping trips round ASDA with Danny screaming and running off. And she worked long hours, cutbacks at the hospital making the psychiatric ward as short-staffed as everywhere else.

He didn't envy her that job, so stressful dealing with all kinds of crazy. Of course she never used that word, she was trained not to. But every time she came back with a story about someone setting fire to their feet or flinging their own faeces around, he ground his teeth together.

'Should we order?' Connie said, lifting a menu.

He looked up. The barmaids were laying out pints in a fluster. Midweek Old Firm cup replay had caught them by surprise.

'Best wait till it dies down.' He looked at the clock. Twenty past seven, kick off soon.

They tried to have a conversation, but the background blether was overwhelming. Nick pictured himself standing up and screaming at them all to shut the fuck up so he could listen to his wife.

He sipped his cooking lager.

They hunkered close against the noise and talked about Danny. How he was doing, whether they should try to see another specialist. But that took months and they were already on two waiting lists. They couldn't go private, barely had enough to pay for two plates of stodgy stew in a place like this.

Nick wondered how Irene was getting on back at the flat. Connie's folks only lived a few minutes away but never offered to babysit, her mum had to be bribed tonight with a bottle of fancy vodka. Connie was the youngest of six kids, so they'd had their fill of grandchildren by the time Danny came along. And all the boy's bullshit didn't endear him to them. He hoped Danny was good for her, or they were never getting out the house again.

'Do you think we should call home?' Connie said. They still had some connection to each other, then.

Nick shook his head. 'If anything's wrong, she'll call us.'

Connie lifted her phone off the table and wiggled it, checking the reception.

The pub suddenly emptied, as if a signal had been given. Two minutes later the barmaids were out collecting glasses. One of them approached. Younger and prettier than Connie. Firmer. Nick hated himself for noticing.

'Are you wanting food?'

They ordered from the menu and another round of drinks. This was on Connie. It was always on Connie. All Nick had was what she gave him. You make up your family unit as you go along, right? If your wife got longer hours and you got the bullet from the engineering works, that was that.

She was well pregnant by then, ready for maternity leave. She went back to work after three months. She had to. He stayed at home and looked after the baby.

It all made sense.

He hadn't realised how it would be, just the boy for company. Four floors up in a shitty flat, in winter too. He spent hours pushing Danny around shopping malls in the squeaky borrowed buggy, just to get out the flat. Looking at things he couldn't afford. In summer he sometimes took Danny along the river, but the combination of decay and sterile rebuilding was just as depressing.

Their food arrived. Lamb in sauce and beef in sauce. Nick ordered another pint, Connie declined. His vision was getting fuzzy round the edges already.

Celtic fans staggered past outside. They'd missed

kick off.

He never understood sectarianism. The Glasgow media were all over it, but people outside the city couldn't give two shits about Catholic versus Protestant. Brought up on the east coast, Nick hadn't been aware of any connection between religion and football until he was well into his teens.

The first time they met, Connie's dad asked about Nick's religion.

'I'm an atheist,' he said.

'Aye, but are you a Catholic atheist or a Protestant atheist?'

It wasn't a joke.

They finished their food. They hadn't talked much. After discussing Danny, what else did they have? Nick's brain had been liquefying for years with every episode of Zingzillas or Waybulloo that seeped in.

The pub was still empty. Eerie. Like a post-apocalyptic drama.

Outside he saw a couple in their thirties, no jackets. He had badly drawn tattoos curling down his forearms, she had a thong sticking out the back of her jeans.

They were arguing. They stopped outside the window. The guy held the woman by the arms and shouted at her. She shouted back and tried to squirm free.

He pushed her and she tottered backwards on her heels. He kept pushing until she bumped against the pub window.

Nick looked at Connie. She gave him the stare.

The guy was holding the woman's arms again. Nick

could see his fingers digging into the flesh. Their shouts were muffled by the glass, but they were going for it. She was still trying to get away.

She spat in his face. He smacked her hard on the cheek so the back of her head clunked against the glass.

Nick shifted in his seat and turned to Connie.

'Do not get involved,' she said.

The woman said something else and the guy slapped her again, then he grabbed her hair and pulled her head down so she was cowering.

Nick looked round the pub. The barmaids were cleaning glasses. Two punters at the end of the bar were sipping and chatting. Connie stared at him and reached out a hand.

Clunk.

The woman's head against the glass again.

Nick pushed his chair back. 'Fuck this.'

'Seriously, don't.'

But he was already at the door.

Four more strides and he had a hold of the guy's arm, felt solid muscle under the sleeve. He pulled.

The guy turned. He still had the woman's hair in his grip.

'What the fuck do you want?'

'Leave her alone.'

'What is it to you?'

Nick was aware of Connie at the pub door. 'You can't treat women like that.'

'Do yourself a favour and fuck off back inside with your bird.'

'Let her go.'

The guy released the woman's hair and swung his fist round into Nick's stomach. The air was sucked out of his lungs and he doubled over, choking to get his breath back. A knee smashed into his face. Pain shot through his nose and tears filled his eyes. He staggered backwards. A fist slammed into his ear, which roared with noise, then a punch to the back of his lowered head made his eyes go blurry. He raised a hand to stop the blows, but felt more punches connecting, then a kick to his knee made his legs crumple and his back thumped on the pavement.

The guy stood over him.

'That'll teach you to interfere in other cunts' business.'

Another boot connected with Nick's thigh, just for show.

The man turned.

Connie was still in the doorway of Babbity's.

The man gestured to the woman. 'Come on, darling.'

'Just a minute,' she said.

She approached Nick, leaned over and spat in his face.

'How dare you tell my man what to do,' she said. 'I'm his woman and I'm his to knock about if he wants. Got it?'

She turned and the guy put his arm round her shoulder. They walked off together, didn't look back.

Connie came over and took his arm, began helping him up. He shook her off.

'Don't,' he said.

He felt his nose as he got to his feet. Wasn't too sore,

not broken.

She reached out a hand to his face, but he batted it away.

Her eyes widened.

'We should get you to the hospital.'

'I'm fine.' He looked at the couple, in the distance now. 'Did you hear what she said to me?'

'I heard.'

He shook his head. 'What is the fucking point?'

'I said not to get involved.'

He looked at her. Worry in her face but also something else. Something primal. Disgust at seeing him humiliated. Or was he imaging that?

'I did the right thing.'

'You did the stupid thing.' Her voice softened. 'Let's just get home.'

They paid up, the barmaid silent. As if she was judging him too. He imagined reaching over and pulling her hair, see how she liked it.

They walked home. The streets were quiet, occasional shouts and songs coming from pubs.

Seven minutes and they were there. Fucked up thing about Glasgow, you could go from moneyed niceties to shitehole in a few hundred yards.

Irene was watching I'm a Celebrity with a tumbler of vodka when they came in.

'How's he been?' Connie asked.

'Up and down,' Irene said, necking the dregs of her drink. 'He's a handful, that one.'

She couldn't get her coat and bag quick enough.

Nick saw her to the door. The click of the snib, then a familiar wail from Danny's room.

Nick rested his head against the door and took a slow breath.

'I'll go,' Connie said behind him.

'No, it's OK, I'll do it.'

Connie could never settle him. Maybe because she didn't see him as much. Embarrassing for a three-year-old to still need settling at night.

He went into the boy's room and reached into the cot, stroked his head. Still in a cot and still in nappies at three. Connie came back from hospital with stories of colleagues whose kids were miles ahead. Maybe they were soft on Danny. Or maybe he was just evil.

Nick shushed him, ran fingers across his brow, whispering, calming, voice low and level.

'My want Mummy and Daddy's bed.'

'No, Danny, go back to sleep.'

'My want Mummy and Daddy's bed.' More whiny.

Distraction needed.

'Give Doggy a cuddle.'

They'd never given any of Danny's toys names, just Teddy, Doggy, Duck. The boy was completely uninterested. What fun parenthood was.

Nick felt his body ache from the fight. Re-ran the thing in his mind, thought about what he could've done differently. But there was no winning for the likes of him.

Eventually Danny went over again. Nick continued stroking his hairline for a few minutes then stopped and looked at him breathing. The boy's face was pale in the green nightlight. Bags under the eyes. They were all tired.

Nick crept out the room and pulled the door behind.

He went into the bedroom.

Connie was under the covers already. She pulled the duvet back, displaying herself. She was wearing the polka dot bra and panties she bought herself last anniversary. He couldn't remember seeing her in them before.

His cock twitched. A ghost of old times.

'Come on, Mister,' she said.

She was worn out, but her smile was alive.

He walked to the bed. She undid his belt and pushed his trousers and shorts down.

'Hello,' she said as his cock sprang up.

At least he could still get hard.

'It was pretty hot, seeing you fight that guy tonight.'

She bit her lip and raised her eyebrows as she played with his cock, her other hand rubbing at her panties.

'I didn't fight him, I got beaten up.'

She rolled her eyes. 'Shut the hell up and come here.'

She pulled him down onto her and he took his T-shirt off, saw his potbelly. She flicked her panties off and guided him inside her. He lifted her legs way up, the way she liked it.

They both came quickly and quietly, her first, then him, like they always used to. He pulled his cock out, collapsed next to her and they both laughed. They were close to getting something back.

'I'm yours to knock around,' she said in his ear.

She was playing that game again, mocking the couple from earlier, reaching out to him with a shared joke.

Something edgy like they used to have.

A picture came into his mind, him grabbing her hair and punching her in the face.

He rolled over onto his back and closed his eyes.

But he couldn't get the image out his head.

Hilary Masters | *Pittsburgh*

My grandfather, Tom Coyne, in his quest for citizenship, wanted to join the power of Pittsburgh. He wanted to contribute his energy and invention to that power, but he had to move on, because he found that power to be exclusive, misdirected and made harmful to the very people it was supposed to enhance, to amplify. My search for identity is neither as desperate nor as direct; after all, I am a second generation, and I can afford to loaf a little on the banks of these three rivers. But I am no less mindful of the struggle for identity, for a place on this delta, so in the temporal coincidence some call history, Tom Coyne and I are merely passing through.

One Spring Afternoon
Hilary Masters

Two large photographs hang on our walls here in Pittsburgh, both aerial views of Forbes Field, the old baseball park. One seems to have been taken from a plane and the other from the high tower of the University of Pittsburgh, just across the street from the ball park. On this parapet, students crowd to peer over each other, their hands waving like victory pennants as they try to see the action on the postage stamp size playing field far below. A radio has just reported the news of Mazeroski's ninth inning home run to defeat the Yankees in the 1960 World Series.

The echoes of that afternoon's history have been gradually rinsed away by the prevailing breezes off the confluence of the three rivers that meet at this juncture, and the students who cheered the Pirates from this high balcony have returned to earth and the making of their own life's history. Forbes Field is no more nor the stadium that replaced it, and I sit along the first base line of the new stadium.

Its home plate and the seats behind face the lustrous towers of downtown Pittsburgh; they rise just beyond the outfield and across the Allegheny River as if topped off only yesterday. I hold a warm kielbasa sandwich, smothered with peppers and onions; a paper cup of the local brew, Penn Pilsner, is snugged into the receptacle on the seat before me. It is a bright, warm spring afternoon and

Kathleen is somewhere in the crowd on her way back to me. The game with the Cincinnatti Reds is about to start; a few players are already warming up on the field, and the fresh greenness of the infield looks as though it may have been trimmed by a Northside barber. Life seldom gets better than this.

It was Fitzgerald who identified the pleasant clime of autumn as "football weather," meaning, I suppose, one of those high crisp afternoons with just a nip in its sunshine to suggest a scarf be worn. We attend baseball games these days in all forms of undress but not long ago, suit jackets and four in hand ties were the rule. Old photographs show entire bleachers stapled together by the exclamation points of neckties though the faces of their wearers remain blurs, a chorus of ghosts with good posture. Kathleen's father sits in one of those photographs. He attended the Series in 1960, and she sometimes looks for him but cannot find him. Baseball is a game played in a pasture where memories graze.

The pastoral has been, I think, an important attribute to this game originated by farm boys in the 19th century and played pretty much the same way today but for the regrettable introduction of the "designated hitter" by the American League. This patch of green meadow below, no matter how encased it may become in concrete, pulls at something deep within me to become the source of a relationship measured ninety feet on each side but is yet immeasurable.

We come here to witness the challenge of a lone individual against nine others, and it is a ritual as determined as anything the Greeks may have contemplated. The sound of that bat connecting with a ball the size of a fist sounds like no other—and its ramifications rise far beyond these cement boundaries to affect an entire city, a whole history. One solid smack and the order of the day has been transformed, righted or made worse, and while the innocence of this play may be reproduced , it is never completely ordained. Kathleen arrives happy with her success, a hotdog with lettuce, tomato and mustard. The Pirates take the field. and hope is lifted once more into the afternoon.

The Shoes of Dead Comrades
Jackie Kay

On my father's feet are the shoes of dead comrades.
Gifts from the comrades' sad red widows.
My father would never see good shoes go to waste.
Good brown leather, black leather, leather soles.
Doesn't matter if they are a size too big, small.

On my father's feet are the shoes of dead comrades.
The marches they marched against Polaris. UCS.
Everything they ever believed tied up with laces.
A cobbler has replaced the sole, heel.
Brand new, my father says, look, feel.

On my father's feet are the shoes of dead comrades.
These are in good nick. These were pricey.
Italian leather. See that. Lovely.
He always was a classy dresser was Arthur.
Ever see Wullie dance? Wullie was a wonderful waltzer.

On my father's feet are the shoes of dead comrades.
It scares me half to death to consider
that one day it won't be Wullie or Jimmy or Arthur,
that one day someone will wear the shoes of my father,
the brown and black leather of all the dead comrades.

Sharon Dilworth | *Pittsburgh*

I have lived in Pittsburgh for the past 20 years. When I
arrived the city was still reeling from m the after effects of
industrial decline. While I have lived here a new culture
has emerged. It is now a paradoxical city -- its new economy based on "meds and eds" competes with the legacy of
its working class history, providing the city with its con-
tradictions as well as its sense of place. Its awkwardness
is in many ways it best attributes. There is a great deal of
social fluidity -- one can hang out at the Squirrel Hill Cage
and drink Rolling Rock, then go to the Carnegie Museum
for a black tie benefit and not worry about the incongruity.

The Cousin in the Backyard
Sharon Dilworth

My husband stands to inspect the bird feeder. He's wearing light blue Winnie-the-Pooh pajamas. He found them at Target, not what he had been looking for but they fit perfectly and the price, like everything else in that oversized, overstocked store, was right. On the breast pocket, Tigger and Pooh fight over the 'hunny' jar.

Target, part of the new development that suddenly appeared on the bank of the Monongahela, is a place I refuse to frequent. To build it they had to tear down the Homestead Steel Mill and in doing so leveled Pittsburgh's greatest asset, its history.

I am often accused of having too many opinions and too much attitude, but I disagree; rage is only one emotion.

Listen to how I see things:

Homestead was the site of the 1892 Steel Strike. That's when Henry Clay Frick in an effort to increase profits lowered the wages of his workers. They went on strike. Like all unhappy workers, the men were fighting for a bit of respect, some dignity, better working conditions, more pay, and an opportunity to fill their days with something other than the dark, dank, and dangerous mills. They never thought Frick would hire outsiders with guns to break the stalemate. But that's what he did. The Pinkertons came up the river on coal barges, prepared to take on the steelworkers who lined the banks waiting for a solution to their misery. The Pinkertons were ruthless –a real massacre --which is why Homestead should be remembered with something other than big-box stores. Of course it's being done all over the world. Why should my corner of the globe be any different?

Because.

This is my world; this is where I have to live.

A bit more history – just so you understand the cause of my rage.

Retribution for Frick's sins came later, when the anarchist Alexander Berkman attempted to kill him. The assassination was a failure; Frick lived, returning to work later that same day. Sentenced to fifteen years, Berkman served fourteen – most of it in solitary confinement --before he and his lover Emma Goldman were exiled to the Soviet Union. Years later, when Frick died, Emma Goldman was adamant that Frick was a name history would forget. "He was only part of the passing hour," she claimed. "Generations after us will not idolize the rich. They will understand the importance of intelligence—they will not glorify greed. Our children will remember Alexander Berkman, a man who fought for what was right. "

I laugh. Try getting fifteen people to name the anarchist. Frick's still famous. For eight dollars, you can have a tour of his house. I've been told they still change the furniture wraps just like his maids did when he was alive— once every six months– white for summer, dark green for winter.

The gigantic Steel Mill has been replaced with a Dave + Busters, a T.G.I.F.ridays, a Dick's Sporting Goods

Store, a Bed, Bath&Beyond, an Old Navy, a Giant Eagle, an Eat-'n-Park, and a Loew's megaplex. Another chain opens every few weeks. A plaque at the far end of the strip mall commemorates the strike, but the empty steel mill with the black idle pipes reaching for the sky is a much stronger reminder of what happened. The complex is hugely successful, though I can't see how that's possible given the stagnant economic and demographic situations in Allegheny County.

My husband, Sam, turns on the TV. Without cable, we get three channels. He watches Public Television and this half-hour is Mr. Roger's Neighborhood. His bowl of Cheerio's, too much milk, the big spoon, and I think, god we haven't come that far, when I see my cousin the backyard.

"I am just not in the mood," I tell Sam.

Maggie is in her lawn chair, the big yellow tent is in the far corner, a make-shift clothesline already filled with her socks and undies. Her shaggy dog Spot barks at the squirrels.

"Lock the door," Sam says. The Cheerio's box is empty. He cuts out the coupons off the back and puts them with the others in the junk drawer.

My cousin sees us. She makes some sort of motion with her hands. I think it has something to do with the bird feeder.

Sam interprets. "Coffee. That's what she wants."

The pot's almost done dripping.

My cousin is an outdoors freak. She doesn't like walls or roofs, or any kind of permanent structures, and has arranged her life so that she's not inside for very long. When employed, she's outdoors: bicycle messenger, hotdog vendor, ticket taker at exit five on the Turnpike, because she believes being inside does funny things to a person's psyche. She's not antisocial, just messed up.

I bring out two mugs of coffee. Maggie thanks me, then peers in over the rim.

"I don't like cream," she says.

"I can't take it out."

"Next time." The sweetness of her gratitude is fleeing.

"Next time, go to Uni-Mart."

She grunts and swallows her coffee in two gulps.

"Where have you been?" I ask. Last I heard Maggie was in Banff, working as a lunch lady at one of the ski resorts.

"The Appalachian Trail," she answers.

"Did you walk it?' I ask.

"I did."

"The whole thing?" The weeds in the driveway grow at an alarming rate. Someday they will probably take over the whole backyard.

"Do I look like I walked the whole thing?" she asks.

She looks tattered, and smells like campfires.

"It's not attractive to always say what's one your mind, especially if it's your mind," Maggie says.

I haven't said a word, but Maggie tells me she knows what I'm thinking. "Since when is honesty considered a vice?" I ask.

"If you're going to be like that," she says, "then I need money." She gives me the empty coffee mug.

I don't think I look like anyone's maid. I hand it back.

"I want to go to France," Maggie says. She puts her feet up on the side of the tree. They are swollen, and her toenails rimmed in black dirt. She probably did walk the whole Trail.

"Paris is where most of us want to end up," I say. I quote something I read somewhere once. "Twenty-two percent of Americans dream of dying in Paris." That doesn't sound right. Maybe I'm confusing it with another statistic – maybe it's 22 percent of the American people can't name the capital of France. They believe Paris to be its own country. Maggie's decisions aren't usually so typical.

Emma Goldman, my lifelong hero, was someone I discovered in grade school, someone I idolized her ever since I learned that we shared a birthday, a religion, and a dedication to commit great deeds. That was how she defined the life a revolutionary – someone unafraid to commit great deeds. I embraced her commitment, embracing it as my life's vow.

The strength of the message, Goldman believed, was in the drama of the act. Violence was not out of the question for Goldman and her compatriots but there had to be reason for any bloodshed. They did not do things without reason, without real purpose. They were not frivolous or self-serving.

Try getting anyone in my life to agree to that. I laugh again.

Sam comes out with more coffee. He's changed out of his Pooh pajamas. They're hanging on the back of his bathroom door. He's afraid to wash them, that they'll lose that soft new feel. They were $7.99. I tell him to buy a dozen. If it makes him happy to have soft cozy, cheap light blue pajamas with familiar animals in bright primary colors dancing about, why not just fill the drawers? Emma Goldman knew that real revolutionaries lead lonely lives. She didn't mention they married men who do embarrassing things that get them arrested --their names printed in the local newspapers. Sex is not something that should be paid for in leafy city parks where undercover policeman are trying to keep the areas clean for young children. Show me the nobility in that act of defiance. It's desperate without thought or conviction. Sam wants to tell me his side of the story as if that would help me understand why he did it.

Maggie wants to know what her chances are that we'll let her camp out in the backyard all winter.

"Nil," Sam says. The bird feeder is empty. Sam re-fills it with a special blend of peanut butter and nuts – pricey items he gets at the Co-op.

"I won't be a problem," my cousin insists.

"You already are," Sam says.

Maggie studies him carefully, hissing a bit, a balloon losing air. "Watch yourself, Sammy," she warns.

Sam's not staying. "I won't be late," he says. He

leans over and makes a noise near my ear, like he's kissing me goodbye. I pull away. Unless we have a good reason, we don't touch. He hurries away, as if late for an appointment.

"Everything okay with Sammy?" Maggie asks.

I tell her she spends an enormous amount of time worrying about other people. "I don't want to talk about it."

"You never do," Maggie says. She gets up to check the clothesline. The sun is warm, but her things aren't dry.

"I am not alone," Maggie tells me.

I think she's talking about the dog. "The neighbors will complain about the barking," I tell her.

"Besides Spot," she says. "I brought a friend."

I walk over and open up the tent flaps. A head, blankets, the smell of someone in a deep sleep.

"She's Malaysian." Maggie says. "I met her in Tennessee. Her name is Aisah."

"Is there something going on between the two of you?'

"I knew you'd ask that."

"Does the answer change because you have ESP?"

"She's just a nice person who needed help. You don't have to be all suspicious and weird just because I'm doing someone a favor."

"Where'd you find her," I ask.

"On the Trail."

"Did she walk the whole thing?"

"I don't know," Maggie says, drinking from my cup.

"We never talked about it."

"Something seems to have tired her out." I take back my cup, but her lip marks are all over the rim. I let her finish it.

"She's a terrific sleeper," Maggie says. Turning the attention spotlight towards others is a developed trick with Maggie. She's more comfortable when she's talking about other people, so I hear all about the Malaysian's sleep patterns. The Malaysian, it seems, can sleep through everything -- Spot's yaps, thunder storms. Why once, she even slept while a group of drunk tourists from Muskegon came to their camp begging for food and drink.

"An incredible mettle," I comment.

"She speaks six languages. She's smart. Really smart."

"And you just found her on the trail? Like that?" Just like that. Walking ahead of you? Talking all those languages?"

"Including Mandarin. She helped out some tourists. They were from India, but somehow they had Mandarin in common and she helped them with their lost passports and credit cards."

The words rush out of Maggie like water rushing over a precipice. She's unsteady and I watch her carefully. Finally she stands and announces that she has to use the bathroom.

"I know exactly how much cash there is in my wallet," I tell her.

She's gone five minutes. I am just about to go in and check on her, when she walks out --one arm slung around her head.

"I saw a bat in your house," she says.

The bat is not usually around in the daytime. The bat flew in last fall and though we've tried everything, we can't get rid of it. It hides from us, slips in, flies around at night. We shut the bedroom door, so we're not bothered, but I hear it moving about the house. It hit the mirror once; the impression of its body is outlined on the glass.

Maggie's made another pot of coffee. She fills her cup, doesn't offer me anything. Five minutes later, she's drunk the whole thing. We stare at the tent and I guess we're waiting for the Malaysian to wake.

Maggie's mother, my Aunt Velma, is slightly paralyzed from the stroke she suffered when the bullet moved through her body. When people ask why she limps, Aunt Velma tells them it was a boating accident.

Long before shooting your parents became a sort of a de riguer act of wealthy suburban malaise, Maggie's twin brother, Jack, shot their mother with a hunting rifle. It's not really fair to blame Maggie for her eccentricities.

Aunt Velma is my mother's sister. They grew up together in Pittsburgh, took dance lessons from Gene Kelly and talk about him as if he still contacts them from time to time. They went to Margaret Morrison College for Women and majored in home economics. They had classes back then like "Dinner for Two on a Shoestring Budget." You should see the way my mother can fold sheets, even 100 percent cotton. She's amazing when she cleans the kitchen -- even disinfecting the sponges when she's sanitized the counter tops. The two sisters married within six months of each other-- my mother to a man so similar to her own father, they even shared first names. Uncle Max was different. As my mother used to say, he had a wider wallet than most of the men they dated.

Aunt Velma and Uncle Max live on Northumberland Avenue in one of the grand old homes that were built when Pittsburgh was a prosperous and opulent city. Drive by now and you'll see street after street of wonderful brick homes with stained glass windows and porticos, front porches, and guesthouses. It wasn't restricted to one area – Squirrel Hill was just one of the good neighborhoods. Most never needed to regentrify; the neighborhoods remained strong even during the recessions of the '70's.

The house on Northumberland was a magical place – a gigantic house of dark wood, secret passageways, hidden closets, back staircases, uneven floorboards, blood red drapes, window seats and panes of locally made stained glass that told stories of turn-of-the-century families. The upstairs had views of the hills and houses beyond our neighborhood. It was dusty; the rooms were filled with over stuffed furniture. Always untidy, the place overflowed with pretzel bins, cases of soda-pop, glass containers for hard candies, stacks of newspapers. They were Russian boxes filled with cigarettes, safety matches, and postcards from around the world. Language records were stacked on the stairs, along with unfinished needle-pointed pillowcases and abandoned jigsaw puzzles.

The family gathered at the Northumberland house for all holidays and Sunday dinners. I remember summer nights as one long continuous party as something or another was always being celebrated.

I drive by the house occasionally, though I usually try to avoid it. The memories are so fresh in my mind that I have to stop the car and wait until the dizziness in my head stops and my vision clears.

In Aunt Velma's words, Maggie and Jack were golden-haired children of God. "I'm so lucky," she used to say to my mother. "They're gorgeous, like movie stars. How can it be? What did I ever do to deserve them?"

Uncle Max and Aunt Velma were proud of the twins and didn't care who knew it. They bragged, way before bragging about your kids was what people did to fill the silences of the day. Maggie and Jack were perfect -- not just stars but starlight. They were playful, enthusiastic, and always good-natured. They were curious and kind, funny, energetic, and engaged. They were, of course, loved by everybody.

I was too infatuated to be jealous.

Jack and Maggie liked having people over and were always in their rooms, in the pool, planning the next party. They were very good at entertaining themselves. They did drugs. They drank. They smoked pot. But they were happy. The house seemed to give them what they wanted. They never complained about the boredom of their lives, like other kids did.

Jack played the guitar and the harmonica and he was always practicing. His favorite song was "Puff the Magic Dragon," and he played it until one of the adults would finally wander over and ask him to stop. "For Christ's sake,

Jack. Isn't there anything else in your repertoire?"

Maggie painted. In her freshman year of high school she started on a mural that was going to tell the story of her life. She was very good with detail and the figures in her mural – mainly Jack and Maggie, Max and Velma -- were miniature. She had tiny slim brushes that she used to paint the exact color of her mother's hair, the right shade for the blue chair in the living room. She spent hours on the mural. It filled her room, the third floor hallway, went around the bathroom, into Jack's room. She had just started on the spare bedroom when Jack shot Velma.

At some point, Aunt Velma must have realized that something had happened to her golden haired, sun-kissed bundles of joy. They grew up to become lazy, sleepy, creatures, who snacked too often, and sipped too much wine from the jugs in the pantry. Their friends were an odd crew of long-haired, mumbling drug dealers. Money was always missing from purses and underwear drawers.

Aunt Velma eventually went on the warpath as if it suddenly occurred to her that her children had become abnormal. She made it her mission to move her kids out of adolescence into adulthood. By summer's end, they were going to be nineteen years old and they were going to be doing something besides sponging off their parents. Maggie seemed to agree – it was time to move on. Jack thought his mother had lost her mind. He went on his own warpath. Since no one talks about it, no one actually knows what Aunt Velma said to Jack that pushed him over the edge, but over he went. Luckily, Jack was too stoned at the time to do much damage. In court he would claim that nothing was premeditated. He just did it. The bullet nicked Aunt Velma's spine, and ended her relationship with her children. Maggie got thrown into the configuration of blame. Neither twin was ever forgiven.

Jack served some kind of juvenile sentence in Bedford, Pennsylvania. When he came back, my father and I went to pick him up at the downtown bus station since his mother no longer acknowledged his existence. My father didn't tell me where we were going – only that he had an errand. We waited inside the car. The heater was broken and little pieces of white paper flew out of the vents.

"I don't want you to tell your mother where we went."

"What should I say?"

He shrugged.

"I'll tell her we went to get a newspaper," I said.

"They never asked him where he got the gun," my father said. "It was the one mystery the lawyers and police never answered. No one knew where it came from."

"Did Uncle Max have one?" I suggested.

"We're Jews," my father said. "We don't own guns."

Then I saw my cousin. He hadn't changed. Like an aura, the goldenness had not faded. I was not the only one staring at him.

They were tears, mostly my father's. I stared at the ground. My cousin thanked my father for coming to get him. "I'm very sorry for everything."

"Everyone makes mistakes," my father said.

"I think this over-qualifies in that respect, Sir."

We got back in the car. Jack turned to me in the backseat. "Hey there," he said and ruffled my head – something you would do to a toddler. I felt childish and stupid. I had expected more from Jack. I hummed Puff the Magic Dragon as if that might bring us back to where we were before he shot his mother. If he recognized the tune, he didn't react. He turned around once or twice and smiled. I felt like a kid trapped in a car seat. But I smiled back. I didn't want to alienate him. I loved him.

We drove through the Fort Pitt Tunnel to the airport. My father asked how he was.

"Fine," Jack said.

"In good health?"

"Very good," Jack said. "Except for the hiccups."

"Hiccups?" my father asked. "Now?"

"I had them last month," Jack said. "For eighteen days."

"My lord," my father said. "That's quite a long time."

All three of us laughed.

"It made me sick," Jack said. "I lost some weight."

"You look like you lost weight."

"I lost an awful lot of weight."

"You look different," my father said, which was exactly the opposite of the truth, something I didn't have to point out. Their conversation was awkward enough without me stating the obvious.

"Do I?"

"You do, I guess," my father said. My father was searching to make conversation. There was an awkwardness in their exchange; so many things they were never going to talk about.

I stared at the back of Jack's neck. He wore a leather

necklace, which was knotted at the back. It had worn, the ends curled and circled around the knot, hanging in the front.

I wondered if they had let him wear while he was incarcerated. Did they take his belongings, then give them to him when he was released? I had recently become obsessed with Emma Goldman and I read her autobiography and was fascinated by her descriptions of jail. I wanted to ask how he kept himself busy – it was one of Goldman's biggest struggles whenever she was imprisoned.

"I wouldn't know, sir. They weren't any mirrors where I was," Jack explained.

"No mirrors?"

"Not a one, sir," Jack said.

"I didn't know that," my father answered.

I wanted to tell him there was a mirror under the visor right near his head. If you slid it open, yellow makeup lights flashed on. My mother kept it down continually when we drove. She inspected her face and throat for new wrinkles. She did her lipstick and complained that her pallor made her look like a senior citizen.

We pulled up to the curbside check-in. I had assumed we were going to go in and walk Jack to his gate. Whenever relatives left, we always watched their planes takeoff. My father got out his side of the car and Jack got out his side. They were hugging again. They were more tears, mostly my fathers.

Back in the car, my father smashed his fists against the steering wheel. "Maybe some of us have guns, but we don't point them at our mothers and pull the trigger."

The Malaysian wakes just as Maggie tells me she's exhausted. "All that coffee gets to me," she says.

"Can you entertain Aisha?" Maggie asks.

"My juggling is a bit rusty."

Maggie gives me the thumbs up. "You can do it." She pulls the lawn chair over to the far corner of the yard and sleeps, the dog's head is on her lap.

The Malaysian has a pack of Drum tobacco and rolls her own cigarettes. She flips out the paper, sprinkles a few strands of tobacco, then rolls it once and licks the ends to seal it. She hides the pouch into the folds of her sweatshirt as if she's afraid I'll ask to bum one. We don't speak, but she stares at the sky every time a plane flies overhead. She smokes one after another, furiously. The smell gives me a headache. I give her my coffee cup and tell her to use it as an ashtray.

She looks at me in confusion.

Evidently, English is not one of the six languages.

I pantomime putting out a cigarette and repeat the word, ashtray several times. "For your ashes," I say. "Ashes."

The Malaysian shrugs, then strains to see a hospital helicopter fly by.

You're doing a good job," my cousin shouts.

"I'm too old for babysitting," I tell Maggie.

The Malaysian brings out a bag full of lollipops. Unlike her precious cigarettes, she offers me one.

It says cherry on the wrapper, but tastes of mothballs. I toss it over towards the sycamore.

I go in the house and she follows. I turn on the television. Elmo and the gang are singing about bubbles in the bathtub. She flips stations, the same three over and over again as if we have 100 channels. She sticks with Elmo.

Seen as a threat to the American way of life, Emma Goldman and Alexander Berkman were exiled to Russia in 1920. Hailed as heroes by some radicals, the rest of this country just wanted to be rid of them and were happy to see the last of them. Carnegie and Frick are celebrated heroes. Their stories are whitewashed in the history books, which ask children to glorify their actions. The anarchists are remembered by only a few, even contemporary historians don't give them much credit.

Sam is home.

He looks out at the yard. "A good thirty minutes and this place will be back to normal." He doesn't like the way the clothesline is wrapped around the sycamore. "The bark is shedding," he says.

He's introduced to the Malaysian who asks if she can take a shower. They go upstairs and I hear him in the linen closet getting clean towels. He comes down and drinks a tall glass of the iced tea. I watch carefully.

"We should talk," he says, but I shake my head.

"Not to worry," I say.

"Really?" he asks.

The groan of the water moves through the pipes overhead. I look to the ceiling. We need to paint.

"Maggie's leaving," I tell him. "She's found the money to get to France."

"Isn't she fortunate?" Sam says.

"I'm not sure I'd go that far."

I used to have a limit at the ATM machine. I'm not sure when it stopped, but I can transfer large sums from savings to checking with a tap of the keys. I grab the dog leash.

"I'll take Spot," I say.

"You don't solve anything when you throw money at her," Sam says. He knows I'm not just walking the dog.

I ask him if he wants to come along.

"I'm okay here," he says.

It's an offhand comment and will probably turn out to be true. But who's to say? Misfortune strikes in an instant. Ask Aunt Velma. According to the horticulturist who came to help me with the fall flowers, the sycamore in the backyard is two hundred years old. My cousin is not stable and that Malaysian smokes like a chimney.

It works like that. One minute, you're an abundantly loved child, with rays of light and warmth reaching down to you, the next your brother's got a gun aimed at your mother's head. Then it's over. The passing hour. You sit in other people's backyards trying to be social so they'll give you money, but you don't really connect. It's not a life, but it looks like one. It's not a life. It doesn't even look like one. It's not enough just to have history. There should be a future; there must be the promise of a future.

The revolution isn't everywhere. It hasn't been in Pittsburgh in nearly a century, not since Berkman came with his revolver, his poisoned blade, and his goal of violent and in retrospect, misguided righteousness.

I'm not giving up – I'm not going to abandon the cause just because I've been tossed a few obstacles. I am the spiritual daughter of Emma Goldman, a rebel in my own right, but no one said I had to stand in place looking backwards and glorifying the past. Great deeds – now.

I go quickly.

Richard Wilson | *Glasgow*

"Glasgow is a great city. Glasgow is in trouble. Glasgow is handsome. Glasgow is ugly. Glasgow is kind. Glasgow is cruel. Some people in Glasgow live full and enlightened lives. Some people in Glasgow live lives bleaker than anyone else should live - and die deaths bleaker than anyone should die."

- from 'Where Greta Garbo Wouldn't Have Been Alone', *Surviving The Shipwreck* by William McIlvanney

The Old Firm and Glasgow
Richard Wilson

One midweek night in April 2011, hundreds of Celtic supporters gathered outside the club's stadium in the east end of Glasgow. It was 11 o'clock, the sky was pitch black and any spring warmth had long since seeped out of the air, but a number of them still wore the short-sleeved green-and-white hooped football jerseys of their team. Word had passed around fan websites, social networks and through conversations between friends and family that they were to meet at the steps in front of the main doors, near a statue of Brother Walfrid, a Marist monk who founded Celtic. In a matter of hours, the crowd had grown, driven by a sense of duty, a need to be there, at the ground - their home - and among each other. The talk was murmured, soft but certain, and the mood was determined. They were there to honour and support one of their own, and they ranged from schoolchildren to people of retirement age. Male, female, rich, poor, the only distinction that mattered was that this was their community, their people, and they stayed long into the night. They were holding a candlelight vigil, and there was a sense of communion.

The gesture was in support of Neil Lennon, the team's manager, who had been sent a parcel bomb in the post. Unlike most of his predecessors Lennon is a symbolic figure: a Catholic from Northern Ireland who is capable of being combative, self-assured, and blunt. To a small minority of hard-line Protestants in Scotland Lennon represents an archetype of what they stand against. Earlier in the season, Lennon and two other Northern Irish Catholics who played for Celtic - Paddy McCourt and Niall McGinn - were sent bullets in the post, while parcel bombs were also sent to Paul McBride QC, a high-profile Catholic lawyer, Trish Godman, a Protestant MSP who supports Celtic, and Cairde na h'Éireann, a Republican organisation in Glasgow.

To Celtic fans, this was an attack on their identity, the Irish, Catholic heritage that remains one of the defining influences on the club. The threats were the work of individuals who held extreme views but Scotland, and Glasgow in particular, still struggles to come to terms with a history that includes hostility towards Irish Catholic immigrants who travelled across the Irish Sea in search of work. Inevitably it also became a football story, since the sport is present in every corner of the city, as if ingrained. Here, not liking football, and not taking a drink, instinctively prompts suspicion: what's wrong with you, son?

Glasgow is a football city, there is a deep reverence for the game and an obsession with all of its nuances; it is reflected in every surface, in every conversation. There are three major stadiums, Hampden, Ibrox and Celtic Park, and only one other city in the world also houses three grounds that can hold more than 50,000 supporters – but that is Istanbul, with a population of 13m compared to the 600,000 people who live in the city of Glasgow. The game is also a form of communication, it is the connection between parents and their children, between men who would otherwise still be distrustful of open sentiment, and is in the midst of every bar room chatter: are you a Rangers man or a Celtic man? One of them or one of us?

Other cities on the north west coast of Britain received the same influx of Irish Catholics and Protestants in the late 19th and early 20th centuries, but none remained so divided for so long. In Liverpool and Manchester, the football clubs cannot be identified as the sole property of one religion or another. Just as the Old Firm benefitted from this tribalism, so they maintained it. Most of the old certainties have passed on, but? Rangers ended decades of an unwritten policy of not signing Catholics when they bought Maurice Johnston, the former Celtic striker, in 1989. The club has since had Catholic captains and a Catholic manager, and the worst of the old songs began to die out.

Celtic are the club with the predominantly Catholic support, Rangers are followed mostly by Protestants. It has been that way since Celtic were formed in 1888 to help the poor among the Catholic community and to keep them from turning to soup kitchens run by the Church of Scotland. Maintaining the faith was a vital concern, and something that is still reflected in the way football affiliations are passed down through generations of families. Rangers were already established, having been set-up by in 1872 by four men - Moses and Peter McNeill, two brothers, and Peter Campbell and William McBeath - in Govan, on the south side of the city, across the River Clyde. The club had no religious affiliation, but Scotland is a predominantly Protestant country and as Celtic immediately began to achieve success (after poaching some of the best players from Hibernian, the Catholic team already well established in Edinburgh), Rangers became their spiritual as well as local rivals.

There was satisfaction to be found in hatred, but also commercial benefits. The two clubs began to thrive in a way that left every other team in the country in their shadow; even now, they are the most successful teams in the country by a significant distance. The two communities were well-defined and their teams were a source of pride, of distinction, of selfhood, so that each began to cling to the other. Commitment became an obligation and there was no greater accolade than being a good Celtic man or a good Rangers man, with the dual meaning that you were also a good hater of the other lot.

The rivalry has been subjected to outside influences. When Harland and Wolff, the Belfast shipbuilders, opened a yard on the banks of the Clyde in the early 20th century, they brought Protestant workers from Ulster who generated a greater emphasis on Loyalism - support for Northern Ireland's continued union with Great Britain - among the Rangers support. Over time, there has also been the steady erosion of the kind of attitudes that saw Catholics barred from certain jobs and professions in Glasgow. By the first decade of the 21st century, the number of active participants in religious ceremonies in Scotland was in decline, and the number of mixed marriages between Catholics and Protestants had never been higher.

Other aspects of the identities of the two sets of fans were also shifting. Where once Rangers were the Conserv-

ative club, and Celtic's followers were mostly Labour supporters, the Scottish National Party were in Government.
Unionist and Republican songs and paraphernalia were
more present at Ibrox, the home of Rangers, and Celtic
Park than ever before, along with Northern Irish flags and
Tricolours. Irish folk music is even played before Celtic
home games, where once that was never the case.

There was a sense of Celtic supporters, many of them
fourth generation Irish Catholics, reaching back for that
part of their heritage, feeling the confidence and the urge
to celebrate where previous generations sought to fit in
or to suppress that aspect of their identity, so that their
connection with Celtic became a displaced form of self-
expression. This might be typical of immigrant communities, the eventual reclamation of their past, but it also
prompted a greater passion for the unionist/Protestant
features of the Rangers identity among the Ibrox club's
fans, many of whom still follow the long-held tradition
of travelling to games from Northern Ireland. Glasgow's
industry, its society and, most enduringly, its football, has
been shaped by this tribalism of Protestants and Catholics;
an antagonism given expression and intensity by the Old
Firm rivalry between Rangers and Celtic.

It is enduringly passionate, with a fiercely contested
pride, but there have been moments of desperation and
stark violence. Ibrox saw two disasters, when supporters
lost their lives, the second of which came in 1971. At the
end of an Old Firm game, 66 Rangers fans were crushed to

death when people left the ground at the end of the match. The surge of the crowd down a steep bank of stone steps to a narrow gate was compounded by somebody stumbling or falling, leading to a press of supporters collapsing forward. In the silence – as the air was pushed from people's lungs – the only sound that could be heard was the jarring creak of metal crush barriers being bent and twisted out of shape by the weight of the crowd. People were trapped, unable to move, and afterwards shoes and jackets were found at the side of the stairway, having been sloughed off in the crush. It was a cold, foggy afternoon and when Willie Waddell, the Rangers manager, and Jock Stein, his Celtic counterpart, climbed to the top of the stairway to see what had happened, steam rose from the still warm bodies.

The tragedy united the city in a shared sense of loss, but it could only be a brief intermission. The Scottish Cup final of 1980 ended in a 1-0 victory for Celtic, after extra-time, but then the two sets of fans invaded the pitch and embarked on running battles. It began with Celtic supporters clambering over security fences onto the pitch, then a handful goading the Rangers fans on the other side of the stadium. Drink, as always, had been smuggled into the ground, usually tucked inside flared trousers, and the mood was violently hostile as Rangers fans charged onto the field. In the middle of the pitch, there was a melee but with an aggressive intent. Opponents could only be identified by the football tops they were wearing or the scarves round their necks or wrists, which wafted in the breeze as men hared around. Bottles flew overhead as punches were thrown, and a newspaper photographer was struck on the head by one heavy glass bottle. The only sound that broke through the shouts and yells of the drunken mob was the heavy thud of hooves as mounted police arrived to break up the fighting, including one female officer on a grey horse who was later applauded off the field by fans still sitting in the main stand, and who burst into tears in response. One of the consequences of the riot was a ban on the sale of alcohol at football matches that still persists.

Players, too, are incited by the antagonism of the rivalry, the constant presence of a sense of rancour. Chris Woods, Terry Butcher, and Graham Roberts of Rangers, and Frank McAvennie of Celtic, all ended up in court after a tempestuous Old Firm game in 1986, while Paul Gascoigne, the Rangers midfielder, received death threats after during a game mimicking playing the flute as a symbol of Orange Walks, which commemorate the July 12 anniversary of the Battle of the Boyne in 1690 when the Protestant Prince William of Orange defeated the Catholic King James, and are still held across Scotland and Northern Ireland. Such a gesture is understood by both sides to be inflammatory towards Celtic fans, although Gascoigne did not know this when he first made the gesture (only to then repeat it again during his time at Ibrox). Players are either inspired or intimidated by the pressures of playing for the Old Firm, the constant need for victory, to stay ahead of the others, to be on top, but some become so immersed that they grasp on to the prejudices, too.

Contemporary Glasgow, where shipyards and tenement housing have been replaced by a service economy

and a sprawl of suburban neighbourhoods, can never release its past. There remains a dark, almost bleak, but sharp
sense of humour that is grittily working class, a strong understanding of social value, and also a quiet pride in the
worth of education and the arts. In an increasingly secular
society, where religious intolerance is no longer considered acceptable, the sectarian language of elements of the
Old Firm rivalry seems a grim reminder of old prejudices
and ancient ideas. Sectarian banners would not be permit-
ted at games (fans have to receive the approval of club
security officials by showing them their banners before
matches), but an edgy wit is often present: "Trophy Cabinet For Sale, contact Neil Lennon"; "The Pope's Goalie"
for Artur Boric, a Polish goalkeeper who was once charged
with breach of the peace for blessing himself in front of
the Rangers fan at Ibrox then making provocative ges-
tures; "At Least John Barnes Could Rap", which Rangers
supporters made for Tony Mowbray, whose Celtic side en-
dured as hapless a series of results as the team managed by
Barnes; and "What's That Coming Over The Hill - HMRC
Want You", which Celtic fans raised after Rangers landed
in tax trouble.

The enmities run deep, but they are mostly now re-
served for show. At derby matches between the two sides,
the hostility is real enough, but what is being expressed in
the songs and the tribal defiance is a football rivalry. There
is never any violence on the terraces now, with the matches being stringently policed. The noise is brutally uncompromising, an exhortation that rise and falls not with the
flow of the match, but the chanting between the two sets

of supports. Being in the midst of the crowd is to be lost to this communal spirit of aggression and defiance, a heart-felt sense of belonging. Everything is a contrast, so when the Celtic fans hold their scarves aloft, pulled straight across, when they sing, "You'll Never Walk Alone", so the Rangers supporters twirl there scarves in response. It is pageantry, but with a hard, vital edge. This sport, that was once so working class that matches kicked off at 3pm on a Saturday afternoon to enable workers to leave their morning shifts and head straight for the local stadium, has now become shaped by capitalist imperatives; money has both enabled the game's expansion but also corrupted some of its ideals. There remains, though, something brutal in the machismo of the terraces, where offensiveness is a form of language in itself, of one-upmanship between opposed sets of supporters.

The acrimony of the Old Firm is typical to football, but the religious element makes the Rangers/Celtic rivalry unique. Ibrox supporters used to sing chants like "Fuck the Pope", "We're Up To Our Knees In Fenian Blood" and "No Pope Of Rome", while Celtic fans sang "Fuck The Queen" and glorified the IRA. Most of these taunts had fallen away, but Celtic were resurgent under Lennon, who prompted a bald hatred among Rangers fans. He is an uncompromising man and has faced a number of unpleasant moments in the city, including being attacked, but the parcel bombs were a separate act, distinct from football. Yet Old Firm matches had become inflamed once more during the 2010/11 season, when the two sides met each other seven times. One match saw a series of players sent off, a typically belligerent mood among the fans, and ended with Lennon and Ally McCoist, the Rangers assistant manager, having to be hauled apart on the touchline. They were lost to a brief moment of antipathy, that creased Lennon's face into a snarl, and there seemed, in the constant skirmishing, a return to the fixture's most volatile nature.

The traumas around the game - Strathclyde Police report a spike in domestic violence incidents after Old Firm matches and accident and emergency departments across the city brace themselves for a rise in the number of casualties in the hours following the matches - caused Glasgow to embark on a bout of self-reflection. In the way that Lennon coped with the disturbances to his life, stoically, defiantly, the Celtic supporters found a cause to gather behind and there was a sense of renewed attachment to the identity of their club.

There has always been a rhetoric of antagonism: Celtic fans would claim they reacted to the intolerance of Rangers fans, a naked anti-Irish Catholicism, while Rangers fans would point to the use of terms like Hun and Orange Bastard as the demonisation of Protestants. It is an endless cycle that seems beyond the reach of the modernising of Glasgow, the departure from the old city of the industrialisation years to something more modern and vibrant, more self-aware, but also more self-conscious.

There were decades when Rangers fans could count on the triumphalism of their club, and its place in the establishment alongside the courts and the Church of Scotland. These were men, and eventually women, who would follow their fathers into a trade and assume it was a job for life. Most of those certainties had disappeared by the time Rangers suffered a crisis 10 months on from the vigil outside Celtic Park. That identity of the Ibrox club's support, the sense of entitlement, had begun to diminish, and leave behind angst.

Under Sir David Murray, the club had enjoyed years of sustained success, but the final decade of his ownership saw bouts of reckless spending generate an unsustainable debt that reached at one stage more than £80m. He also authorised the use of Employee Benefit Trusts for discretionary payments to players that were tax free, only for Her Majesty's Revenue and Customs to decide in 2010 to claim back taxes retrospectively. By the time the debt had been pared down to £18m in May 2010, the club was also in the midst of a tribunal with HMRC that could potentially deliver a bill of up to £50m in taxes and penalties.

When Craig Whyte, a businessman with a vague background and an unconvincing manner, bought the club in May 2010, it seemed momentarily like a release from years of downsizing and fretting. Yet nine months later, after a bout of ruinous financial vandalism, the club was placed in administration, owing a further £15m to the tax man and still awaiting the verdict on the use of EBTs. There was a serious prospect of Rangers being liquidated and the assets - the stadium, the training ground and the players - being transferred to a new company. This would be a separate legal entity, and so represent a break from the previous 140 years of the club's history. There was always an air of superiority in the way that Rangers fans claimed the team's 54 titles to be a world record, and the sudden threat of this primacy being undermined was un-nerving.

Older supporters were aghast at the prospect of the institution they had grown up understanding to be digni-fied, proud, upstanding, not paying its taxes. While Celtic fans were gleeful, and adopted songs like, "jelly and ice cream while Rangers die" to express their own triumphal-ism, the Ibrox support had to rally. There was a brief out-break of angry defiance when some old songs referencing Fenians were heard during the first home game after the club went into administration, a 1-0 defeat to Kilmarnock, but the response was mostly heartening. The stadium was full that day, home to a surging, almost visceral pride, and supporters gathered outside Ibrox in an act of communal faith and hope, as if standing together would, alone, be enough to ward off the worst fates. Banners proclaimed their unending loyalty to the club and although the tone was occasionally sombre, the instinct was to be blunt and uncompromising. The team must not die, they said, we can't let it.

Fans turned out in numbers, they set up a bank ac-count for donations that would be used to help pay running costs, they launched a new range of scarves in red and black, the colours of Govan, as a fundraising initiative, and began campaigning for fan ownership or at least a role in the governance of the club once it emerged from admin-istration. This was an act of renewal, of Rangers support-ers reconnecting with the old ideals of clubs being funded by their supporters, of the very act of commitment being central to the team's success. The players also made sacrifices, with the entire squad and playing staff taking pay cuts to allow the team to complete the season. The higher earners agreed to a 75% reduction, the middle earners to 50% and the lower earners to 25%. This was an unprecedented gesture in football, but a measure of the depth of feeling for the team. Many of the players and staff grew up Rangers supporters, and the club was already under the skin of the rest. There was moral piety from the Celtic fans, but also the sense among Rangers followers that the club had to learn lessons from its financial collapse, that responsibility had to be taken for its future wellbeing rather than waiting, passively, for a benefactor to realise their ambitions. Just as Celtic supporters had been energised by the defiance and protection they offered to their manager the year before - "We are all Neil Lennon," became a recurring phrase - so the Rangers fans had to respond to the sudden decline of their team. The two sets of circumstances, coming so close together, began to appear like a test of devotion, a scrutiny of the role the two clubs still play in the lives of the communities that follow them.

There are still Rangers areas of Glasgow and Celtic areas, Rangers pubs and Celtic pubs. Even education is segregated since there are non-denominational state schools and state-run Catholic schools. It is the two football clubs that now represent this old divide most clearly, but also the spirit of unity that gathers around them. They are social institutions, locked in an endless, futile even, tussle for football supremacy. Glasgow still suffers from poverty and gang culture, from communities of listless people, unemployed and vulnerable to drink and drugs, who will live off benefits, but also has many areas of wealth and privilege.

It is a fractured city, yet the most enduring divide of all is also, in many ways, a reflection of a shared understanding. The Rangers and Celtic supports are drawn from the same socio-economic backgrounds; religion apart, they are the same people, with the same spread of hardship, affluence, ignorance and education. Football binds them all together, even if it then immediately reinforces their segregation so that many Rangers fans wear Northern Ireland strips and many Celtic fans wear Republic of Ireland strips to games.

The troubles of Northern Ireland never carried across the Irish Sea, but attitudes did. They remain present now, but mostly in football chants: Celtic fans singing The Boys of the Old Brigade, a Republican favourite, and Rangers fans singing Derry's Walls, a Loyalist song, as if Irish history was still deeply relevant to these two Glasgow clubs. There are periodic moments of calm in their rivalry, and then sudden outbursts of renewed hostility, but what endures, in the love of the game that is an abiding part of the city's heritage, is the understanding that the two teams matter.

They draw individuals together: 60,000 at Celtic Park, 50,000 at Ibrox. There is no more thrilling football spectacle than a game between Rangers and Celtic, and no rivalry that could be reduced to such small mindedness as the Old Firm conflict. They now win all the championships between them, and their fans compete on every multi-media platform, only further prolonging the sense of combativeness. As Glasgow has moved on from its past, the football of the city remains rooted in its old certainties and is, with the continuing devotion of one generation after another, endlessly contentious.

There is also a deep sense of pride, though. It is estimated that 80,000 Celtic fans travelled to Seville for the 2003 Uefa Cup final, while upwards of 150,000 Rangers supporters went to Manchester for the 2008 Uefa Cup final. These mass movements of people were manifestations of the cultural, social and emotional importance of football to the city; the game's place as a fundamental characteristic of being Glaswegian.

From that night at Celtic Park in April 2011, Celtic fans adopted a saying: We Are All Neil Lennon. It was meant as a statement of comfort for their manager, but the vigil that spring evening and their emotional response to the intolerance Lennon faced, was as much an expression of what Celtic means to them. In this city, the two main football teams are more than clubs, they are a way of life.

Yona Harvey | *Pittsburgh*

Power and Possibility	04720
The Black Interior	15559
The Black Automaton	19342
Black Nature	08203

That
Yona Harvey

I grew up with pickles. I slept in
the attic (cigarettes, sheets laced with
smoke). The heat of my father's
brother's old room. Larry Blackman
painted for effect & Chaka Khan's lips
more like a kiss if a kiss could walk
when it came to life. If a kiss
could have hips & legs & ass—
well, I wanted that.
& if the colors could sweat & strip
me down to my slip, well,
I wanted that, too. Nobody knew
what I was thinking up there.
Though, maybe, they wanted that. That.

Ghosts of Mount Auburn

She reins the frame, my father's
mother. She guards her teeth, her
vagabond daughter, & vaulted

chambers with a gun-cocked stare,
with her finger pointed. At you.

At me. At my sister knocking.
She wants to return to her
rightful place. But she cannot.

Go back. (My sister? My father's
mother?) She's waiting for just
the right record to sing, the paws

on the stairs, the bark, the beg,
the jingle on the collar. All dogs sit
without her asking. Her fa-la-la-la.

Her fa-la-la-la. Where did she leave it?
Talbotton, Georgia? She can't go back:
the cigarette pocks, the beer bottled

drunks. Good and gone like
Gluttonous Sunday. Like cousins
with chill and lyrics verbatim.

What was that song? What was that
glare? Point. Shoot. Trip the shutter.
Her eyes are half-open. Her slip

strap is showing. Her hem is hanging.
My children can see it. My father, you can
see it, too. She wants your admission:

You left the door open. You lost
your daughter: my sister. My father,
her one steady verse, her—   fa—

la-la-la. My children: they're singing.
They can go back.
Weather the whether. Or wither or

not. The manual camera doesn't
go back. Smile? Forget it (for now).
Forget it. Her eyes are open.

She's through talking. (My sister?
My father's mother?) She's out
of the frame. Good graces?
Good God? Coulda stayed

in Georgia. (Maybe God's
in Georgia). Wait for good—
whether—   Wait. Fa-la-la-la.

Posting Bail

Keep missing me, you say. *Armchair, stepstool, tree stump, church pew*, I'm thinking up a list, half listening. Sit back & hold still, I tell you. My list is lacking. Sooner or later, I say, you'll come up on the Sheriff. & by April, the Bondsman on the fourth floor. *Sofa, swivel, chaise.* He'll be waiting for the right answer, some hint of repentance or pencil-skirted decorum, of a straight-backed, arm rested, ghost of a former teacup tipping self. *You'll have to meet*, he'll say with a twist of his belt, *certain conditions.* You'll think of your cousin by marriage then. The one who insisted you "meet certain conditions." The one who wanted so badly to act like a man. *Call this number & that number on this day & that. Then maybe I'll help you*, your cousin by marriage said. Apparently, men make ultimatums. & operate under certain conditions. & look women in the eye & say, *be more professional*, like your cousin in manface. Like the Bondsman. *What's my deadline*, you mutter to no one in particular, hoping to change the subject, leaning back in your chair.

Q.

One of the four Royal Stars is watching over me. Yeah, I'm blessed in these times of nervous weather. The leaves chill in a bundle then scatter like police, off to the next doorstep. They don't step, they don't phase me. These jeans could hold three men. But it's just one of me, girl. Only Son. Only Sound. Only Seer. All this green to gold to red to orange is just theater. I'm the Real. Keep your eyes on the Navigator of Snow and Infinite Gray. I rock these boots all year. What a storm got to do with me? Who knows the number of strolls to heaven? Not that I'm thinking on it. The Heavens know my real name. But you can call me Q. Quicker than Q. But, anyway. Certain things a man keeps to himself. Jesus wept. So I don't. The past is for people who like to play things over and over. Me, I'm on to the next song. Listen to my own Head Symphony, to the Royal Stars. The colors, they thrill me, they fuel these legs. The weather, the weather, the music.

Jane McCafferty | *Pittsburgh*

East Liberty, 1986: Trains ran through my back yard. I wrote on a typewriter in the tiny kitchen before sunrise. Headlights of the train streaked across the page. Somebody was always heartbroken or going crazy and it always rained. One day we discovered an old church blasted open, statues standing in the rubble. On the South Side, one of Pittsburgh's last steel mills lit the sky with fire. So many unemployed men in the bars, so many shops, all of them old, none of them gentrified. You could talk to old people from Eastern Europe, mentally ill people, and mentally retarded people, all of whom seemed at home on those streets back then. In Oakland the old blind black guy would sit and sing gospel music with his boom box. Helicopters landed on the roof of Children's Hospital, and the sound meant a child was near death, which had a way of putting things into perspective.

Little Tasks of Life
Jane McCafferty

For years I went with my husband John Clarence (may he rest in piece) to Tessaro's on Thursday for ravioli. I especially loved it in the winter. To slip into the dark tavern, sit in an old booth, and smell the marinara sauce while snow drifted down through the dark behind you in the window, it was something like heaven. We were regulars, along with Frank and Doris Brennan, Marie Romano and her daughter Peg, Jimmy Savoy the electrician, Jimmy's sweet sister Clare who wasn't right in the head, and Father O'Neill, the old pastor at Immaculate Conception. Father O'Neill and Johnny loved to talk Irish history. And we all loved our waitress, Ruth, as so many did. She wore a look on her face that seemed like a long thank you for the wonder of this strange life.

I'm usually not one to grasp the wonder. For me it comes in small bursts, like the time I saw a blue heron standing in a river. Or in the old days, when I'd hear my daughter singing on the sunny mornings, a wee child in the bath.

Or five months ago when I found my husband dead in his armchair. You'd think I was the only person to ever have found her husband dead in his armchair. I mean to say it was such a shock—that I could lose my husband when he was just 69 years old—you'd think such a thing had never happened before on this earth. I kept trying to wake him up. For the longest time. Then I sat in the chair beside him, waiting for him to wake. The night before he'd talked to me about wanting to learn to play the banjo. I don't mean to tell you it was all perfect with us. But we'd been the kind of friends to who had a lot of laughs together. We'd been the kind of friends who spent most of our days looking forward to the evenings in our house, or down at Tessaro's.

I stopped going after he was gone. I tried to avoid all our haunts, which was difficult given the length of our marriage, but especially I avoided Tessaro's, which he loved most. I missed the other regulars, I really did, but I couldn't face them. I listened to my cousin Beverly's advice. "Stay busy." "Find a new hobby." "Maybe learn to knit." I did learn to knit. Maybe I made myself useful by producing decent enough scarves for the homeless women down at Bethlehem Haven. When I wasn't knitting, I was working my usual job behind the snack counter at the hospital with Joyce, the talkaholic type who can take a half hour to tell you her experience of watching a late night television commercial. Beverly said to give myself a gold star every time I made it through an hour. Visualize the shining gold stars all over your body, all over your mind, your heart, your soul. When you're covered with them, start putting gold light in the air around you, and all over other people. I did this each day. Now visualize blue stars, she said. Blue light. Ok. I would've done anything she said.

Then I'm walking down the street last Tuesday and I run into Maxine, who used to groom our dog way back when, and she says did I hear about Ruth from Tessaro's tragedy? Ruth's son was killed in a car accident ten days ago. He was driving with some kid who just got his license. The kid was speeding down the parkway and lost control of the car, and Ruth's son went through the windshield. The driver survived but Ruth's son Cal died in the ambulance.

"Is Ruth still at Tessaro's?" My face burned, remembering Ruth and her son at John's funeral. He was a handsome kid, dark haired, unguarded. He'd embraced me in his white shirt and striped tie. And he and Ruth had stopped by one night, a few weeks after John died. I looked out the window and saw them on the steps that night and couldn't find it in me to open the door. I didn't want to fall apart on such nice people.

"Oh yes, she's still there."

"Is she doing all right?"

"God, who knows."

Maxine was in her mid-seventies, she was known for her beautiful garden with its huge statue of Saint Francis, she had nineteen grandchildren, most of whom showed up for Sunday dinners. She was the sort of person I'd always wanted to be. She lived off of Liberty Ave, not far from Tessaro's. Sometimes I'd convince Johnny to stop and say hello to her after we ate there.

"So anyhow, you might stop in and see her," Maxine said. "She's asked about you several times these past months. They all miss you down there."

I sat in a booth far away from the booth where I used to

sit with John. Still, it was not easy to be there. But if Ruth could lose her only son at age fifteen in a car wreck and keep waitressing in the wake of what they say is the worst grief in the world, I could certainly survive sitting there without my husband. Ruth approached my table, stopped in her tracks when she saw it was me.

"You! Where have you been?"

I didn't answer that. I just said it was good to see her. That I liked her new red hair. She stepped forward. I studied her face for a moment. She'd lost a lot of weight. Her eyes looked too big.

"Ruth I'm so sorry," I said, and reached out my hand, which she grabbed onto and squeezed. "I just heard the news yesterday or I would've been here sooner." Her eyes were lowered, but when she opened them wide and looked at me, I felt a kind of electric shock go through my body.

"So what can I bring you, Love?" My husband always liked how she called people Love. When he suffered a depression one year, Ruth was one person he wanted to see. Because her happiness contained sadness somehow. It wasn't the kind of happiness that's so fragile it recoils from someone else's pain. It contained the whole world and all its ruin. So if you were depressed, it didn't make you feel more alone to be around her happiness. Because you were in it. You were part of the happiness and so was your horrible psychic pain.

"The usual ravioli," I said.

"How are you surviving?" she asked me then.

"The question is, how are you surviving?"

"It's like each moment is a fist punching you hard

right here," she said, pointing to the space just below her breastbone, her eyes blazing. "We're like those stunned boxers who just stand there and take it. Right?"

"Because what's the alternative?"

"We can't leave the ring. No, no no."

"No, we can't."

"Because we'd be setting a bad example for other human beings," she said. "My customers would never forgive me."

"Right."

"We want to stay right here in the ring and do our thing," she said, and I could hear some anger in her voice.

"That's right."

"God's with us," she said. "God's with us in all this shit. Don't forget that, Love."

"So Ruth, you're faith's unshaken?"

"Stronger. How would I get out of bed with a dead son if I didn't have some kind of faith?"

I just kept looking at her.

"Faith that he's somewhere being loved and taken care of, faith that I'll see him again? How would I live without that?" Again I heard some anger, and her eyes flashed down on me. I wanted to stand up and hold her.

"I don't know, Ruth."

"Anything to drink? Some Merlot?"

I nodded. She scribbled on her pad. And before she looked back up at me she reached way down deep inside of her soul, and brought up a familiar light into her face for a moment.

When she moved away I looked out the window. Ear-

ly Spring, a lavender twilight, a kid in a red jacket standing on the corner looking lost. He was a beautiful boy. I
saw him as Ruth would see him—a version of her son.
Then I turned around and watched her wait on another table across the room. I could see her profile. I could see
her eyes lighting up as she spoke with the little girl at
the table. I could see her nodding, and then she laughed
a little, talking to them as she wrote down their orders,
one of her white sneakers poised on the toe of the other
one, her dyed red hair pulled back away from her face. I
felt I could have watched her forever. She was both herself and all the people in this world who keep on moving,
keep on performing these little tasks of life, even when
their own hearts are shattered beyond recognition. They
remain here like ghosts, working to find their traction, and
they do find some, and they find it with grace, don't they?
And those who don't, I understand them too. And as Ruth
turned from those customers back toward me, and walked
through the dim light of the restaurant toward the kitchen,
she looked over, caught my eye, and winked.

Louise Welsh | *Glasgow*

Glasgow is the place where I live.
I have lived here for a long time.
Sometimes I hate it, sometimes I can think of nowhere finer, mostly it's okay.
I don't have to live here, but I do.
Glasgow is the place where I will die.
I'm hoping this will happen around 2055, but statistics suggest it may
be sooner.
Of course I may not die of natural causes. I could be hit by a bus, a
Glasgow bus. Glasgow bus drivers have a habit of reading the Daily
Record when they're driving, and I don't always pay attention when I
cross the road, so it is not out of the question.

No Jetpacks, No Future?
Louise Welsh

Travelling the motorways that slice through Glasgow it sometimes seems the only glimpse of the past is the in reflection the rear-view mirror. We're driving in the future, through a JG Ballard-concrete-dreamscape sprouted with tower blocks. Freeze frame and it might be a modernist triumph, but hit the play button and it's quickly clear this isn't the future we were promised, and it's not just jetpacks[1] that are missing.

There are moments, in the middle of the day, when you can see what the city planners were thinking of (apart for those alleged brown envelopes) slick autobahns speeding citizens to high rise heavens. But mostly these days, it's a snare up. No one is 'stepping on the gas'. We're all in our separate pods, singing along with the DJ's choice, or learning Spanish, Italian, Portuguese; always some sunny language. Steer down into the city though, and it becomes a different story.

Don't get me wrong, this place is up-to-the-minute, up-to-the-second. Our fashionistas can skate all the way down Hope Street on five inch heels without the aid of a cardigan. We get our sushi straight from the conveyor belt and all the biennales in Europe can't contain our avant-garde. But Glasgow is a town where the past is always present.

I have a map on my office wall headed, GLASGOW

CITY CENTRE EVACUATION ZONES. Do all councils issue these, or are ours especially vigilant? The River Clyde lies beyond the boundary that designates the central zones, so the map only shows a pale blue glimpse, as it curves along Clyde Street then down the Broomielaw. The mapmaker is right. The Clyde is no longer the centre of this city, but it was.

In 1707 the Union of the Crowns opened up English colonies to the Scots and the Clyde got busy. It was too shallow to negotiate ships into the middle of Glasgow, but it flowed into the North Atlantic Ocean. From such accidents of geography great fortunes are made. Ships sailed for the Caribbean and the Americas, trading in cotton, sugar, rum and tobacco, transforming Glasgow from an underweight town into the second city of the empire. Traces of the trade remain. The merchants liked to splash the cash, as keen to show off their wealth as a city banker driving a four by four. They erected grand mansions and trading centres, building themselves into the fabric of the city.

John Glassford is one of several tobacco lords with a street still named after him. Glassford Street is in the heart of the city centre, not far from Buchanan Street, named for another tobacco merchant. You can see a portrait of Glassford and his family in the People's Palace. It's nicely composed, Glassford and the other grown ups seated while the children play around them and in the corner, almost painted out, stands an enslaved African servant. Jamaica Bridge was not named after the old music hall joke[2]. The slaves did not go to the plantations of their own accord.

We didn't build this city on rock and roll.

The merchants' trade was triangular. Goods went to Africa where they were exchanged for newly enslaved people who were then taken to America or the West Indies and forced into work on plantations. The products of the slaves' labour, sugar and tobacco, were then brought back to Britain.

Glasgow's tobacco lords might just as easily be called the slave lords, they profited on all three legs of the journey, and their profit was dependent on human misery[3].

The Clyde made Glasgow and Glasgow made the Clyde. The river was dredged, docks built, jetties constructed, tributaries diverted and finally, when the industrial revolution arrived, the Clyde was deep enough to take advantage. Heavy industry replaced trade.

I've lived here for twenty-five years, but I could have been Glasgow through and through. My great grandfather worked in the Clydebank docks. He got involved in politics, became part of Red Clydeside[4], was blackballed, went down to England for a while, then snuck back up to Edinburgh where he found a new trade, and kept his head down.

He would have approved of the fitness freaks that pound the river's banks now and of the new bridges that span it shores, but he'd notice an absence; Henderson's of Meadowside, Stephen's of Linthouse, Fairfield, Clydeholm, Inglis, Blytheswood, John Brown's, Beardmore's and Connels. From the 1840s shipyards started to appear along the Clyde's banks. The yards were booming, but the workers were still broke.

Poverty, desperate living conditions and opposition to World War One helped politicise Glasgow. In 1919 the government was so certain the city was on the brink of a Bolshevik revolution, they ordered the Highland Light Infantry to be locked in their barracks at Maryhill, and deployed around ten thousand English troops. Glaswegians still talk of the day Winston Churchill ordered armoured tanks to roll into George Square[5].

Shipbuilding was hit hard by the great depression of the thirties. Clydeside remained red, but it was another war, rather than the labour leaders, that resurrected the yards. Along with Liverpool, the Clyde handled most of Britain's merchant shipping during World War Two. But the boom came at a high price. The Clydebank blitz lasted for only two days in 1941. But when it was over only seven houses were left undamaged. Fifty-three thousand people had to leave the district and hundreds were dead.

Wars help industry and for a time in the fifties shipbuilding on the Clyde continued to flourish, but by the mid sixties the industry was in decline. Some ships are still built on the Clyde, but by the time I came here in the mid 1980's it seemed to me that Glasgow had turned her back on the river, almost as if the city couldn't bear to look at it, now it wasn't pulling its weight.

In a country full of hills, it's nice to find a flat path, and so I often walk the city stretch of the Clyde. The river has changed a lot over recent years and my route takes me past the headquarters of STV and the BBC, massive digital centres constructed from steel and glass, part of a development that includes the Science Centre, an Imax, the Armadillo and the Scottish Exhibition Centre. Not far away is the Riverside Museum, a shiny tidal wave, devoted to transport, and designed by iconic architect Zaha Hadid. Lately modern apartments have sprouted along the river's banks, white Toblerone prisms, luxurious and balconied. Nearby new stadiums are being built in time for the Commonwealth Games in 2014. We're told that this is part of the Clyde's next phase, a multimillion pound regeneration that'll bring new jobs in its wake and turn the walkway into a centre of commerce and leisure.

I want it to work. But, like the drivers snared in the slow moving traffic on the no-longer-a-motorway that scars our city centre, I can't avoid glancing in the rear view mirror. I keep glimpsing the past, and the ways the Clyde generated the wealth that helped form this city.

It makes me wonder what this chapter means for the citizens of Glasgow. Will the river serve new generations well, or will the profit from new Clydeside developments be confined to the spiritual descendents of tobacco merchants, slave traders and arms manufacturers, while the great granddaughters and grandsons of shipyard workers wipe café tables, sweep floors and operate the tills in the museum gift shop?

Dusk comes in. The cars stalled on the expressways turn on their headlamps, and form into shining necklaces of lights. Back when the future was bright, squads of high rises would have shone too, as near to New York as some of us would ever get, proud and starry ribbons. But they're coming down now; failed experiments and controlled explosions, leaving an absence on the skyline.

I want the glossy new Clydeside the prospectuses promise, I want luxury flats for all, mass communications and sunshine on the water. I want to see the pilot of the seaplane tipping his hat to pretty girls in summer frocks as he lands safely, near the water-skiers who are zooming through the surf. I want decent homes and jobs that give satisfaction. But I can't rid myself of the conviction that it's the past, rather than promises, that offers a window on the future.

> *I backwards cast my e'e,*
> *On prospects drear!*
> *And forward, tho' I canna see,*
> *I guess an fear*[6]

1. We Were Promised Jetpacks are a band based in Glasgow.
2. My wife's gone to the West Indies.
   Jamaica?
   No she went of her own accord.
3. Further information about Glasgow's involvement in the slave trade can be found in, It Wisnae Us, The Truth About Glasgow and Slavery, Stephen Mullen (RIAS, 2009)
4. Popular name for mass radical socialist movement associated with the Clydeside which sought to improve the living and working conditions of workers and their families c.1910-1930.
5. Winston Churchill, much admired in the rest on Britain because of his role as Prime Minister during WWII and his association with victory over fascism, is still unpopular in Glasgow due to his decision when Home Secretary, to send tanks into the centre of the city in 1919, in a bid to break a general strike demanding a forty hour working week.
6. Robert Burns, To a Mouse

Psychic Spiritual Adviser to the Stars
Lori Jakiela

Gina pulls up in her black Volkswagen, reaches across and gives the passenger side door a shove. "You look like crap," Gina says to me. "Sally will know what to do."

Sally is Gina's psychic. Gina is taking me to see Sally as a welcome-home gift. Gina thinks this is a good idea. I do not, but because Gina means well, I try to be open.

A trio of Virgins dangle from Gina's rearview mirror like a tiny ballet troupe, their feet pirouetting on snakes. A blue statue of Mary bobs on a spring on the dash. Around Gina's neck there's another small gold Virgin, a St. Christopher medal and a red Italian horn. The whole car smells like vanilla air freshener and peppermint gum. New Age music clinks around on the stereo. The music sounds like coins being dropped by handfuls into a metal sink. It's meant to be soothing, like rain maybe, but it isn't.

I buckle up and check my face in the visor mirror. Gina's right. I look like crap. I look like someone who hasn't been sleeping. I haven't been sleeping. A few days before, I fell face down on the sidewalk. I had not been drinking. I had not been dizzy. I had not tripped on any discernible thing. I had just gone down flat on Carson Street, right beneath the sign for Jesters

Tattoo Shop. Jesters' logo is a laughing devil in a flaming jingle bell cap. There is still gravel in my chin. My right hand is scabbed over. My right shoulder aches.

Gina flicks her mirrored sunglasses onto her head, slaps the visor up, and says, "You won't be sorry."

Ever since I moved back to Pittsburgh in Spring 2000, I've been a wreck. My father is dead, and my mother is heartbroken and sick. She has breast cancer. It's in remission for now, but now her heart, the actual organ, is failing. "A bee's nest," the doctor says. The list of everything that could go wrong is awful – heart attack, stroke, embolisms. "It's hard to say what will happen," the doctor says. "We'll do what we can."

"Do what you have to do," my mother said when I asked if she wanted me to come home.

"We're fine."

After 50 years of marriage, my mother can't give my father up. His death is unthinkable, impossible to translate. When I try to imagine how my mother feels, I turn to words I'd never use for anything else, as if only something as logical as science could hold such sadness. Symbiotic, symbiosis. A molecular, cellular loss.

"It's freezing out," she said the day he died. It was snowing. The wind felt like a slap. My mother tried to stop the funeral director from lowering my father's bronze casket into the ground, like she was worried my father would die out there. "We can't bear it," she'd said, meaning the cold.

We.

There was no we. My mother was alone. She couldn't remember how to write a check.

There were so many pills to take. Some days she

didn't get dressed.

"We do what we can," she said.

My mother needed me, though she would never use that word, need. And so I came. I left my job in New York. I left my tiny rent-controlled apartment in Queens. I left a man I'd been seeing for years. He and I hadn't liked each other much, but it was something. I thought of this move back home as temporary, just until my mother got better, just until things settled down.

That's what I still tell my old boyfriend when he calls now. When he's drinking or lonely, he asks me to come back. "When?" he says, and I say, "Soon." It's an easy lie because sometimes, when I'm lonely or drinking, I want to wish it true.

The first thing my mother said to me the day I moved home was, "Well, it took you long enough." She said, "What did you have to do that was so important?" She ran her fingers through my short blonde bob and said, "You always did look better with long hair."

Then I saw the way her fingers shook when she held a pen, the way her breathing sounded like static when she fell asleep in a chair, and I knew.

When she'd wake, at first she wouldn't recognize me, then she would. She'd say, "oh, you're home," like I'd never been gone long, like all this time I'd been out for milk and a newspaper, like all this time she'd been here, waiting.

I've always loved cities, but I loved Pittsburgh, my home city, first.

As a girl, I'd hop the bus that stopped outside my house in Trafford, a tiny mill town 17 miles outside of Pittsburgh proper, and take it downtown. My mother would worry, but she'd let me go. A little freedom developed character, she thought, so sometimes she forced herself to say yes.

The bus stopped and picked up at the McDonald's on Forbes. I knew my way to the Point, to that place where three rivers came together. I knew the fountain. I loved to sit there and watch the incline wobble up Mt. Washington. The incline is red and black. It looked, still looks, like a ladybug.

I don't remember how old I was for those first bus trips, but I must have been very young because the mills were still going. I'd come home and the collar of my shirt would be filthy. I'd blow my nose, and the tissue would go black with steel dust. "Jesus, Mary and Joseph," my mother would say, blotting at my face with a tissue she'd wet with spit. "Just like your father."

My father would come home covered in graphite. For over 30 years he breathed it in, all that black metal. It's what killed him.

Still.

The city was, and is now even more so, beautiful. There are glass skyscrapers that look like ice castles, like something Superman would hide out in, but my favorite is the Grant Building, a simple thirty-three stories. The lights on top of the building are a flashing beacon.

They're supposed to spell out Pittsburgh in Morse Code, but as a girl I thought they spelled "I love you." The lights are red. They look like a lit cigarette. They look like a beating heart. A while back, a retired pilot translated the lights and found that they really spelled out Pitetsbkrrh.

Maybe this way, the wrong way, is prettier.

Sally the Psychic is in Butler, Pennsylvania, just outside of Pittsburgh. Butler is not a city. It's not the kind of place you'd expect to find a psychic. Butler is the kind of place where you'd expect to find cows. Tractors and slag heaps. You can get great cabbage in Butler. The whole area is pretty, if you don't mind the smell of manure. There's a lot of patchwork farmland to ogle, and I bet somewhere, in some little diner run by an old woman in fuzzy slippers and a housecoat, you can get a great slice of pie. I just can't figure out who, other than Gina, would travel miles of rickety back roads that seem paved with corn to get advice from someone who, in her off hours, sells cat paraphernalia at a store called The Country Kitty.

"Sally's an expert," Gina says. "Womb-regression therapy. She can take you back to before you were born. You can see where things went wrong."

An ambulance races past as Gina turns towards the Turnpike and Butler. I feel my breath catch. Every time I see an ambulance, I'm sure it's my mother. "It happens all the time," the funeral director said after my father's wake. "One goes, then the other."

Whatever our problems, my mother has always made

it clear she loves me. And I love her, desperately, in the way that daughters with fierce mothers often do. I can't separate my life from hers.

"When you lose your mother," a friend told me, "you have to re-make yourself."

I can't understand this. I never want to understand it.

An hour later, we pull up to Sally's house. There's a sign nailed over the porch. It looks like something a kid made in woodshop, ragged letters burned into a piece of driftwood. The sign says Psychic Spiritual Counselor. It says, Walk-Ins Welcome. There are no neighbors.

Sally hears us pull up and comes out. I've only seen city psychics before. They always dress the part – lots of heavy jewelry, maybe a bandana. Sally is wearing cut-offs, a wifebeater, and a pair of old boat shoes. She has long blonde hair that frizzes in the humidity. She is tan and pretty and completely un-psychic-looking.

"I'm so glad you made it. Gina, honey, my computer's acting crazy. Maybe you can take a look? It keeps flashing on and off. Like it's possessed," Sally says and giggles. She waves her tiny ring-less hands next to her face, like possessed jazz hands. Then she turns to me.

"I'm so sorry. Let's go in and have some tea," Sally says. "Gina honey, I hope you can get that old computer up and running. You're good with those things. You have a gift. I've got my life in that computer. I mean, my life. Everything."

I think someone with psychic abilities should have the foresight to backup her computer files, but I don't say so.

The kitchen is filled with copper pots and dried herbs.

On the counter and sill, there are ceramic cats. The cats are playful – one with a ball of yarn, one licking a paw, one tipping over a little carton of milk. On the refrigerator, there is a large star-shaped magnet. The magnet's glittered message: "Psychic Spiritual Adviser to the Stars."

"We'll just settle in," Sally says. "Then we'll see what we can see. Do you want sugar?

I'm not supposed to have sugar. Screws up my perception. Caffeine, too. But I love it. Sugar and caffeine. My two main food groups."

When Sally laughs, she makes a little yapping sound. She finishes with the tea tray and we go back to the computer room. Other than the computer, a card table, and one folding chair, there isn't any furniture. There are a few pillows on the floor. Sally and I sit on these. Gina tinkers with the computer until Sally's screensaver, a picture of lions in the wild, stops flashing.

Gina fiddles some more, then hits the volume button. A tin version of the theme from "Born Free" cracks and chirps.

"You are a genius!" Sally says. "I've been saved!" She begins singing.

I am glad for Sally, glad her computer has not eaten her life like a nit. But she's brought a deck of tarot cards on the tea tray and I'm waiting for her to pick them up. She doesn't. She and

Gina make computer small talk instead. I try to drink my tea. It's herbal. It tastes like licorice and pond scum. It tastes medicinal, like something my mother might have forced on me as a child. "Just hold your nose and drink," she'd say and push the cup to my lips. "You want to get better? You have to help yourself."

A few moments later, mid-sentence, Sally stops talking. She looks at me and says, "Well then." She eyeballs me in a way that feels probing and intense and psychic-like. She says, "Close your eyes," and I do, even though I've always hated closing my eyes in front of other people. It makes me feel vulnerable.

"Relax," Sally says. Now that I can't see, her voice seems different, deeper, steadier.

"Breathe," Sally says, and I breathe, deep and full, a good patient.

I know now what I want, why I'd agreed to this. I want a diagnosis and a cure, whatever way it comes. Gina has her dashboard virgins, her medals, her New Age hope. I'm not sure what

I have. The priest at my father's funeral had held my hand. He'd said, "Pray with me." But I couldn't. I couldn't even open my mouth.

"In. And out," Sally says.

I feel myself float. My lungs fill and roll like waves.

Soon Sally will tell me that Armand, the spirit guide she'll summon up for me from the other side, says I should take vitamins and get my eyes checked. She'll say Armand wants her to tell me I should take up painting and possibly ceramics. She'll say Armand worries about me. He thinks I'm not in touch with my spirit animal, which, according to Armand, is either a rabbit or a wolf.

"Armand says you're confused," Sally will say, and shrug. Mid-session, Sally will pull her hair and break down weeping over her own failed marriage, her rotten husband who's taken most of the furniture and sent her business belly-up.

"Never trust a Leo," she'll say between sobs.

But in these first few moments, with only the sound of her voice and my breathing, Sally gives me something and I'm grateful.

"I want you to visualize," Sally says. "Let the images come."

For what seems like a long while, there's nothing. And then there is a face.

It's an old man I'd seen the day I'd fallen in front of the tattoo shop. He seemed drunk, like he just left a bar, but he didn't stagger. His steps were careful and sure, like he'd been doing this for years. He was dressed in work clothes, the way my father had dressed – a faded blue shirt and worn jeans, steel-toed boots, a handkerchief in his side pocket. He may have just been getting off night trick. He may have stopped for a few beers before heading home.

"Ah sweetheart," the man said. "Took a dive now?"

I expected him to help me up. Instead, he stepped around me and kept going.

"Don't worry, sweetheart," he said. "We've all been there."

Ewan Morrison | *Glasgow*

MAXIMUM FINE £1000

Scotland will never be free until it learns to pick up its own shit.

Where, Who and Why
Ewan Morrison

So, one of my new year's resolutions was to get out more and I don't just mean the pub, and get Jenna to stay more nights with her dad and the weekends with my mum so I can maybe learn myself somethin for once and no just be sittin round thinkin I'm a goldfish in a bloody bowl or getting pished and wakin up with random guys stinkin up my bed. So anyways, I joins this creative writing class: EXPRESS YOURSELF! it says on the advert on the board, up there with the usuals for second hand motors and baby buggies. I wasny sure but it was just across the way and it was only a tenner and I'd spend thirty on a night out anyways, so why the hell no? Try anything once, me.

OK, sorry. Everythin starts with a Where - that's what Jerome says, he's the weirdy name teacher. The three W's are the start of every story, he says. The Who has to live somewhere if it's going to have a Why. What about homeless folk? I says and he must have thought I was takin the mick, but I wasny. The three W's eh. Wot a woad o wubbish.

Anyways. Where I live.

They've no named my street yet, or if they have no one's telt me. All of it round here, houses and all, was put up by Tesco's. Jerome says we're no supposed to use brand-names in our stories, cos we should be aiming for 'Timelessness and Universality'. And I says to him well there's a Tesco's everywhere I've ever been, like Dublin and what-you-call-it in Slovakia, so ye canna get more universal than that, cowboy. He didny find it funny cos he's a serious bloke and arty. Anyways, he could do with getting intimate with a bar of soap, could Jerome.

Right - The three W's.

I live on the street with no name so if you want to get a taxi to mine, like on a Friday night hunney, after closin time, then all you have to say is Tesco's. Well, the street behind. Take me to Tesco's! It always gets a laugh out the drivers cos ye canny go to Tesco's in the middle of the night, right?

Forget it.

So the community centre – Tesco's had to build it cos of some government malarkey. Anyways, it's this fancy glass-walled thingy over the other side of the car park, with a wee library in it and a tea room and you can rent out the wee hall for five-a-side or meetings but nobody even knows it's there, no even the buses. It's got it's own wee bus stop, brand new, with this empty frame where a timetable should be. One time, I was just off my shift and I sees this old wifey standin there waitin with her shoppin bags and it was going to rain, I could tell.

There's no buses round here Hen, no yet anyways. That's what I says. The road to fuckin nowhere. And it started rainin right enough, but she blanked me like she was feared I was going to mug her or somethin. Silly cow, probably was there all night. Mibee still is - a skeleton.

So, anyways, I'm upstairs in this wee room in the community centre and they've put out a big circle of twenty chairs but there's just me and this old bird and a young Goth guy and scruffy old Jerome, and it's freakin me out, cos of the smell of the carpet glue and the carpet's too clean and fuzzy and probly makes sparks if you walk on it with trainers, just like the dole office when they re-did it. And the seats are like they just had the plastic wrapper taken off of them. Weirdy, like it'd be better if there was some stains or stinks, like damp or something usual, you know? Then there's this classy beige wallpaper and one of those wipey-clean boards with the word 'YOU' written on it. And I'm wonderin if I walked into the wrong class and maybe it's AA or Cancer Support. And I'm hopin someone'll just fart or something.

So I'm planning a quick get away. But then I mind Jenna's at her nana's and it'd be a waste of a night if I just went to the pub, so I gives it another ten. But it's hard no to stare at the folks, so I'm looking out the window. And it's weirdy cos there's these five big windows that go all the way to the floor like a movie screen and there's the big TESCO sign about twenty feet high and right across from us. So I'm sittin there trying to line up the T in one window and the E in the next and the S... you get the picture, and all this red light coming in from the sign, all over everyone. Jerome would probably say 'We were bathed in red light' or 'blood' or some such pish.

- Hello, sorry I didn't catch your name, he says and he has a nice voice. Soft and kind of shy poshy English and déjà vu-like. Anyways, so I says my name and he asks me what I do for a living and I just points at the sign.

- Really, you work in Tesco's? And I can hear the old

dear next to him clearing her throat.

The old dear. Suppose I'll have to do the Who's now I did the Where's. Another thing I forgot was we all had to do wee name badges which was classic cos there was only three of us. Anyways, God's in the details.

So the old dear looks like she's foreign, like Pakistani or Greek, that's my first impressions. Olivey skin and wrinkly hands, you know how they age faster in hot countries. Serious looking, Crabbit my mum would say. She's wearing man's shoes and she doesny care, and those cheap tights we sell in packs of ten. Her name's Sal.

Jerome's telling us all this stuff about the three W's and readin us this story by the Russian guy whose name's kind of déjà-vu too. Then he stops with one of those pregnant pauses and says - So now, it's your turn. Anyways, there's the other guy too but I'll never get done if I start on him.

He says - Now I want to hear about your life. We have to write a page, that's what Jerome says, He goes to the board and rubs out YOU with his sleeve, not a sponge. And I'm thinking, that's a bit fuckin drastic cleanin that green pen off with your sleeve, and he did kind of pause before he did it and look around like he hadn't done this before, I mean a creative writing class. Anyways, he writes - A DAY IN YOUR LIFE - in big squinty capitals and says - everyone is a unique individual in a unique place - All you have to do is describe your daily lives truthfully and authenticity will shine through, or some such. He tells us he wants us to use the three W's, but no to worry so much about the Why, just focus on the Where and Who and how we have ten minutes and he's sorry cos he forgot to bring pens but he has some paper.

I'm thinkin, a day in my life – aye right. I wouldny read that if you paid me. If I'm going to spend time and money readin then I want a bit of romance or a war and all that malarkey, like in the past. I mean you look out my window and it's no Doctor fucking Zhivago, that's for sure.

Sure enough, I've got my pen out my bag and my paper and I'm staring out the window and can I think of anything to write? Is the Pope a proddie? So what I end up doing is staring at the Goth guy – he's called Jed – And maybe it's cos time's tickin and I'm gettin distracted as usual but I'm thinkin he's just like my ex, Johnny, when he was twenty He's got that dyed black hair and the torn black jeans and he probably thinks he's Iggy Pop or such-like. And it makes me sad thinkin I fell for all of Johnny's malarkey and he really must've believed it himself cos that's why he ran off. My mum said he's selling flat screen tellies in Comet now, which is not even in the shoppin centre and how he's got another lassie up the stick and still givin it his shite about being a great undiscovered poet. And as I'm starin at this Goth kid's nose ring, I'm thinkin Johnny's well behind in his child support payments and maybe the why I came to this stupid course was to prove I can do the one thing that bastard never did and write just one fuckin sentence.

Four minutes left, Saint Jerome's sayin and I'm kick-in myself for wastin time. I'm lookin at his scrawny hand-writing on the board and the huge sign out the window and

I'm startin to panic so I do the usual – I do my to-do lists.

Get up. Get Jenna to nursery. Get to work. Work. Tea break. Work. Lunch break. Work. I think about the three W's and the Where is just out the window and so it's really just here, and the Who is me and so I'm stuck.

\- You should be finishin off now, ole Jerome says.

The other two are scribblin away. I'm no going to panic I tell mysel. It's no like he's management. I mind that he says you could bring it to life with dialogue, so I tries a bit of it.

Do you have your own bags today? Do you have a Club Card? Please put your PIN number in and press enter. So then I get in on the Where, and start to write about the checkout counter.

The conveyor belt is plastic and black and sometimes it gets stained with milk, or when people put things on that are too tall, like 2 litre bottles of cider or coke, they fall over when the conveyer belt starts up again and the till is just a bit too close to my seat and I'm always hitting myself in the belly with it and I always forget to give them cash-back and have to do it all over again with the supervisor unlocking my till and he's got BO and always leans over me and I'm stuck there between his stinking hard-on and the till, which is pretty much the highlight of my day, and so I have to pack things into the plastic bags but not all of them because if you do it all for them it'll slow you down on your quota.

\- OK, time's up, he says.

Even though there's more to say and I've filled half a page I know it's pure mince cos everyone short of pygmies in the Amazon's been to Tesco's and some things just don't need to be said.

- So who'd like to go first? Right enough, it's the old dear, volunteerin. She clears her throat and stands, her voice is dead professional and she has this accent like a German. She pushes her grey hair out her face a few times.

I woke early and looked out at my white room. The white lilacs sat strong and upright in the white vase. In places the old wallpaper was still showing through the layer of new whitewash and they reminded me of all that still had to be cleaned, replaced, turned to white. In the mirror too, I glimpsed my face, the white hair that I had let grow this last year and come to accept, like the passing of so much.

Sorry, I'm not making this up - we got photocopies of each other's writing – Jerome sent them. They'll never get to see mine though.

In the corner of the room were the boxes I had so carefully packed in the last month, the one stack with labels that read 'Charity', the other that read 'Recycle', the last that read 'Destroy'. I rose to the window and looked out onto the street, its smells washed over me on the first breath of morning air. Freshly cut coriander and roasted cumin and falafel. The street sounds rising over the roofs like song from the synagogue.

Then there's this big silence. I'm squirming and a bit pissed off cos I didny realise you could do it about any day in your life. Like, if I'd known that I'd have done it about my holiday in Naxos. Jerome's strokin his goatee beard and starin at the floor for a minute. Goth boy twitches in his squeaky seat.

- Very evocative, Jerome says, have you done classes like this before?

- This is my eighth class, she says, with this kind of proud old smile.

- Would either of you like to comment at all on the page, Jerome's asking. - Anybody?

And I'm about to say it was like a book and fabby, but she cuts me off.

- It's about the holocaust, she says. Her mother had been a survivor. The white room was a metaphor for healing and forgiveness. She's been working on a novel since her husband died.

Jesus, what can ye say? I'm feelin dead guilty for thinkin she was a Paki. Pardon my French.

- Thank you very much Sal. Really, it was very beautiful, Jerome's sayin.

The red lights are glowin over us and I'm glad cos I must be blushing like a well spanked arse as I'm starin down at my page - The conveyor belt is made of plastic and sometime when milk spills on it ...

- OK, who would like to go next?

I'm prayin for a fire alarm or some shite to go off. Goth boy shuffles on his seat, crosses his legs, and puts his head to the side, all sensitive like. He doesny stand up to speak. His voice is kind of whispery and I'm practically fallin off my seat from leanin forward to hear him.

Making all of the clamour of which I am capable, I break through the brittle vegetation choking this dessicate gully down which the stream is channelled. There are so few leaves to these trees, barren here in the height of summer. I move at the pace of my own time, and relative to actual time it's like the tossing and catching of a coin on a speeding locomotive, me with my time in actual time and moving. I think. There is nothing extant between this time yesterday and this time today: a loop of found film spliced and sequestered, as my history shrugs its scar across the itching wrist of this void.

Man, it's mental and I feel like havin a wee laugh. No that I'm sayin it's pish, it's just, well, like he 's from another century or somethin.

Jerome's strokin his beard and sayin, very rich, very thought provokin, reminiscent of Baudelaire, but you could have done a bit more with the Where and less with the Why. Like, right enough, you ask yersel Why too much and you get nowhere. Story of my fuckin life.

The Goth kid's all curled up on his seat like he's a vampire and Jerome's flashin maybe a bit too much daylight on the subject and I'm thinkin, Oh boy that'll be me in a minute, shite.

Sal clears her throat.

- I'm sorry, but it's pretentious beyond belief.

- Let's try to keep our criticisms constructive, Jerome says.

- You should go to the West Bank young man, then you would see what a void looks like.

Christ, Goth boy is lookin like he's going to pish himself and I'm feelin kinda maternal or somethin to him.

- Well, it's interesting nonetheless, that it provokes such heated debate, Jerome says, and that's the first time

I see his hands are shakin and somethin about him really does give me the ole déjà-vu's.

- Debby?

Sorry, that's my name. Duh! Marks off for the Who.

- Would you like to comment?

Me? I wanted to say it was weirdy and scary and tell him he sounded like he'd swallowed a dictionary but all I says is it was fabby, cos I know what it's like when folk are gangin up and tearin chunks out you. I says I liked the bit about the gully, a whole world in itself - who'd have thunk it. That's me just witterin away like a numpty.

- Great, Jerome says, two very strong pieces - So, last but not least. And then he smiles at me and they're all waitin. You know that thing about your whole life flashing before your eyes before you die. Well, it sort of does only I wasny dyin.

- No, I says, I canna. It's just mince.

Sal touches my knee.

- We all have different lives and it's a joy to hear about people's diverse

experiences.

Jesus, I'm thinkin, well, I'd fuckin love to be able to write about Palestine and what have you and slashing yer wrists but this is just about the checkout counter. I couldny stall any longer and I thought it wouldny be fair if I bottled out since they'd been so brave to read theirs. So, I takes a wee moment and starts.

We had a problem with the scanner today. Sometimes it doesn't work, usually with the reduced items, most it's the cheese and fish and then you have to hit the manual

button and type in the eighteen digits which is hard because if you get one wrong then you have to start again. It
happens a lot after seven o'clock when the reduced items
get put on with the yellow stickers. It's a real pain because
it slows everything down and pushes down the customer
quota, and usually the packing on the reduced items leaks,
especially the meat which is boggin. We get a lot of reduced coleslaw and cheese and onion pasties, fuck knows
why, and come eight I'm sick of typing in the stupid numbers.

There's tons more but I can feel the air's goin all dead
around me, like I farted in church or somethin. Goth boy's
bitin his knuckle. The old wife's starin like I'd just telt her
I had leprosy or somethin. Jerome's lookin out at the big O
of the Tesco sign. I'm tryin no to run out screamin and I'm
starin at carpet, thinkin, it's only half nine, Jenna's at her
mums, time to get back home, get tarted up, down a voddie or three, hit the pub before closin time. I'm tastin it.

- Well, well, well done all of you. Jerome says. Well
done Debby. Does anyone have any comments?

The old woman's straight in.

- Well, I found it all a little abstract. I didn't get a
sense of place. It could have been anywhere.

I'm thinkin, go easy there, hen, I did my best. I'm hot
from blushin and my head's spinnin.

- Aren't there any people in your daily reality, you
seem to be obsessed with products.

The carpet patterns are getting weirdy and I'm thinkin
I'm gonna puke - will ye just shut it.

- I find that very disturbing, you could do with some

details about people, to bring them to life, otherwise it's like, I hate to say it … well, a conveyor belt.

You try servin seven hundred people a day I felt like shoutin, with your supervisor starin over your shoulder. One person every one minute and forty-nine seconds. You can get fired for being too chatty. I'm thinkin maybe a fag would help the puke feelin, but there's no stopping her.

- Surely you must meet all kinds of interesting people of different ages and creeds? You must have some wonderful conversations?

Eh, no really.

Jerome's over there cringin like fuck and Goth boy is like, shootin daggers at her outy his wee vampirey eyes.

Maybe, tomorrow at work, I should, really try to observe people, take it as an exercise, she's sayin with this big smile. Take time to write down my observations. – For example a man with a moustache and a sloping gait; an Asian woman with a pram and lipstick on her teeth - really to work in a supermarket must be a gift to a writer, to study humanity at such close range. God is in the details.

Aye and he's dead and so'll you be if ye dinna shut the fuck up. Thankfully, before I says that, Goth boy cuts her off and smiles at her, which for a Goth is not a pretty sight.

- Actually, I thought it was wicked, he says. You should read some Raymond Carver, he says, he's shit-hot on the pointlessness of existence.

Then Jerome jumps in, trying to be the boss.

- I agree and you should try to write with your native tongue, he says.

What? I might be original but I'm no an effing aboriginal. And I'm thinkin, what's the point of me draggin myself up and learnin how to talk properly if they just want me to write like ahm some fuckin' numpty fae the schemes like, ken . Which I was, don't get me wrong.

I can hear myself breathin and I'm burnin up and gaspin for a fag and so I stands. I cuts him off and just tells him, Sorry, I says, if it's shite but that's ma life - I'm just glad to have a job cos they come and go, like men, like.... and sorry I canna express myself but maybe I havny got one to express anyway, and sorry it's no fucking War and Peace. OK?

They're all starin, jaws on the floor, like loony tunes.

Fuck it, I says, That's all folks. So I'm pickin up my bag and down the stairs and out. It's pishin with rain so I'm round the corner, under the bus shelter, lightin up, blowin the smoke out and lookin at the way it goes round the edge of the buildin and gets lit up by the red light, thinkin aye that's about it, right enough, that's about as close as you're ever going to get to Tolstoy or whoever, ya arse.

But then I hear them outside and Jerome's voice and I'm stuck there cos if I go round the corner they'll see me and then I'll have to say the sorry's and the old dear'll be givin it the sorry's too, then there'll be the goodbyes and Jesus. My feet are getting wet and I keek out and see the Goth boy holdin an umbrella and the old dear under it and headin across the car park to God knows where cos there's no taxis up that way and I'm thinkin, fuckin hurry up, it's pishin and I'm freezin. Then I sees him, he's coming round the corner, roll-up in mouth, Jerome, headin right at me.

-You got a light?

I says aye and he takes it and lights up, then he's just smokin and blowin it and watchin the smoke, and he's no saying nothin and I'm thinkin I should apologise, but then he says.

- You were right.

And I says, Aye a right arse.

No, he's saying. No. He's tellin me what I said was better than anythin he's ever written - the essence of the great untold story of our time. And I'm thinkin funny what a wee bit of nicotine can do to a guy, and it gets weirdier the more he gets serious and I've no idea what he's on so I'm askin him what.

- Contemporary life has become so repetitious and banal that it is impossible to dramatise.

Away and pish, I tell him.

He's standin in the rain, starin at me so hard it's making me feel kind of hot and bothered. He lowers his eyes cos he's got shy.

- When you come back next week, he says, we'll do some work on character, how to tell someone's life from what they wear and how they move, the little things they do that betray their emotions. And even before he's sayin it there's me tryin to read him, like he says, through his clothes and wee moves.

He's about forty is my guess and he smokes a lot cos his suit stinks of it when he's close, and it looks second hand and too short at the sleeves, and he's a bit like Kurt Cobain would've if you made him get a job in Woolies for ten years, but handsome, he must have been. He's playing with his fingers where a wedding ring might have been. His shoes are scuffed at the toes. He has a notepad in his pocket and the bulge where maybe a book or a bottle had been before. His hands are shakin bad as he lifts the fag to his mouth, and that's when I get it. That's where I've seen him before. Cos I never look at the faces. Then I kind of go into this wee dream world.

I check to see if the last one's taken their debit card from the PIN machine and say thanks, then turn to the next. The shakin hands.

Have you got your own bags today sir?

He's not meetin my eye because he's only got one item. It's standin right up and I know as soon as it reaches the end of the conveyor and hits the metal his two litres of Savers Extra Strong Cider'll fall with a thud, and he'll be embarrassed, and there'll be that awkward silence thing until one of us reaches onto the weighing area to pick up the bottle and eyes must not be met and nothing said cos it's only ten a.m and the guy is buying as much cheap booze as he can for his breakfast. He pays by cash, his fingers tremblin. He's not even met my eye and he's walkin away, fast as he can, forgettin his change.

I look up and Jerome's got this needy look in his eyes but I can tell he hasny recognised me. The rain's stopped and I've got some voddie in the flat but I tell myself no to be daft.

- So, will you be joining us again next week? he asks.

I say, naw, probly not, Sorry, it's no my cup of tea.

But the way he looks at me.

I tell him I'll see him the morrow morning and laugh

at my own wee joke. He doesny get it.

In Tesco's, I say, and give him a wee peck on the cheek. I head over the car park, lookin down at the white lines and the red puddles and I'm feelin his eyes on my legs. I look back and he's just standin there under the bus shelter, waitin. Poor Soul. He disny know about the bus stop, probly.

There's nae buses there, I shouts. It's the road to fuckin nowhere!

What? He shouts back.

I know I shouldny and I told myself I wouldny, but he looks like he doesny know where he is and the one thing I do know is that the Who and the Why dinny really matter, if it's just for one night. As I say, it's no Doctor Zhivago.

Come on then, I shout over, ye can get a taxi from mine.

Charlotte Glynn | *Pittsburgh*

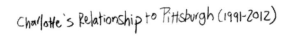

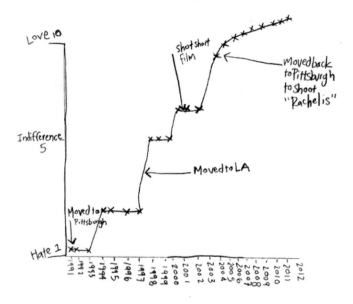

Charlotte Glynn

When my parents told me we were moving to Pittsburgh from outside New York I was excited, a new house, new friends, a new school. All of this vanished on my first day at Florence Reizenstein Middle School, a place straight out of the nightmares adults have about school. It was a hideous, windowless prison of a building full of tough city kids who thought I was totally weird and for the most part were right. I definitely wasn't helping myself fit in wearing huge tinted glasses and fully embracing my love of gingham[1]. Worse than all this was how vocal I was about my hatred of football. In Pittsburgh this is something you just don't do. By the second week of school my excitement became outrage as I realized my parents had moved me from the coolest city in the world to a post- industrial nightmare where the sun only shines 63 days a year and the regional food is the pierogi[2].

As I got older my hatred of Pittsburgh became more profound and time consuming. My joke in high school was, when you say Pittsburgh stinks, you really mean it. By the 90's most of the steel mills had closed but on many mornings you could still smell the ghost of the industry that used to be[3]. As a teenager yearning for the glamour of New York there was nothing worse than being stuck in a dead city, a depressing grey and ugly place. A place so terrible that it actually stunk.

In Pittsburgh football is more than just a game, it's a cultural heritage, something to depend on even when times are hard. In the 1970s when mills began huge layoffs and steelworkers were losing their jobs, the Steelers dominated the National Football League. The Steelers, like the people of Pittsburgh, were famous for their hard-hitting tough defense known as the Steel Curtain. For many people, unemployed and struggling, the Steelers represented something to be proud of even as the industry that created Pittsburgh began to disappear.

As a teenager I didn't care about the Steelers, Pittsburgh's history or why abandoned mills lined all 3 rivers, I just wanted out. As soon as I graduated, I moved as far away as I could. I wanted nothing to do with Pittsburgh and I swore I would never come back.

In my 20s I began to make films and started to think about the stories I was interested in telling. On trips back to Pittsburgh to visit my family I began to see how the history of Pittsburgh and its people is visible in the landscape: the abandoned mills, the libraries, streets and cemeteries. I decided to shoot my first short film in Pittsburgh, a process that drew me closer to the city's narratives, allowing me to see Pittsburgh as a hard-working, misunderstood place, full of secrets, twisty roads that lead to beautiful views, staircases cut into streets too steep to climb otherwise. I began to see the landscape not as ugly and grey, but rich with history.

And then I found myself with free tickets to the 2004 playoff game between the New York Jets and the Steelers.

At this point my close friend was a Jets fan and he made it clear he'd never speak to me again if we didn't go. We drove from New York to Pittsburgh the night before the game. In the morning, bundled in long underwear and ski pants, we made the pilgrimage through the tornado of black and gold clad tailgaters to Heinz Field, the Steelers' stadium. The stadium is situated right where the Monongahela and Allegheny Rivers meet to form the Ohio River. From the end zone where we were sitting I could see the hills of the South Side of the city speckled with tiny row houses, the inclines that used to bring workers down to the mills but are now just a tourist attraction, and the yellow bridges, crisscrossing down the rivers like stitches, weaving Pittsburgh together. It was electrifying, the view, the roar of the crowd, the thousands of fans waving their Terrible Towels[4].

The Pittsburgh Metro Area was still struggling to redefine itself after the loss of the industry that created the city. There weren't enough jobs and many once vibrant communities had become ghost towns as younger generations left home for work elsewhere. But the Steelers were on fire that season at 15-1, a franchise record, with a rookie quarterback who hadn't lost a game yet. Whatever hardship existed in real life was eased by win after win through the fall and winter. There was a tangible sense of euphoria -- this year we'll make it to the Superbowl again[5]. Intellectually, I had always understood that Pittsburghers loved their football, but standing in Heinz Field with 69,000 cheering fans was the first time I actually felt it.

At the end of the 4th quarter the game was tied with a minute and 46 seconds left when Steeler's Quarterback Ben Roethlisberger threw an interception. This was my first football game, I didn't know the rules and barely understood what was going on, but I felt that interception in my gut, along with every other fan watching the game. As the Jets set up for a game-ending field goal, the crowd was hushed, the stadium lights blasted the field, making things look more than real. Time slowed as the fate of the season came down to a single field goal. I looked around the stadium, all the fans standing solemnly, clutching their Terrible Towels, hoping that the season wouldn't end like this. At that moment, as I stood waiting for Jets kicker to determine the fate of the game and the season, I understood that the Steelers had to win[6]. If they didn't, a depression would blanket Pittsburgh. It would be a blow to a city that had already been fighting for so many years. Pittsburgh deserved to win this game. They had to. As I stood in Heinz Field praying for a win, I realized I was part of something, I was experiencing a new emotional territory, one I had mocked as a teenager – fandom[7].

With 6 seconds left in the game we waited, hearts pounding, as the Jets attempted a field goal that would end the Steelers season and crush the excitement and optimism that had built up in the city over the course of the season. I watched as the ball hurtled into the air towards the goal and ... missed. The crowd went crazy as the game went into overtime[8]. Strangers hugged me and gave me high fives. The last remnants of my judgment of Pittsburgh melted away.

To be a fan of any football team is to say you're willing to have your heart broken, willing to stand behind a force that's destined at some point to fail.

So maybe my journey to fandom was inevitable. I love the heartbreak, the intense and unwieldy desire for a win, the neurotic mental replaying of games gone wrong. On the Monday after a bad loss even a stranger at the grocery store will know how you feel. Isn't there some comfort to know you're not alone in this heartbreak? Part of being a fan is the solidarity: you are never alone with your sorrow. What other aspect of life allows for such communal grieving? In Pittsburgh the Steelers have been a glue, the certainty and consistency even as the city has changed. Season after season the Steelers essence has remained intact: they play a hard, physical, smash mouth football.

By becoming a fan my relationship to the city has grown exponentially. We now have a common language, a history, we've felt the joys of winning Superbowls[9] and the crushing sadness of losing the games that we should have won[10]. My friend once described fandom as an abusive relationship, and for him, a Philadelphia Eagles fan, maybe that's true. For me being a fan has kept me connected to a city I have grown to love and respect.

1. I know it's hard to believe I could look like this and be outraged by anything other than my sense of style, but trust me I was.

2. A Polish dumpling. Filled with something savory like potatoes, meat or cheese. They are either boiled or fried up with some onions. Best pierogies in Pittsburgh, if you don't have a Polish grandmother, is probably Pierogies Plus in McKees Rocks, which is on the way to my sister's house.

3. I've been told that it's the smell from the remaining coke plant. (Coke that is used to make steel, not the drug or the soda – or pop as they call it in Pittsburgh)

4. The Terrible Towel was created by Myron Cope, the charismatic radio commentator for the Steelers in 1975 as a gimmick to rally fans. Cope gave the rights to the towel to Allegheny Valley School, a residential program outside Pittsburgh for people with disabilities. Myron Cope and I also went to the same high school along with Wiz Khalifa and Curtis Martin, a former running back for the Jets.

5. The Steelers hadn't won a Superbowl since 1980.

6. Here is my friend the Jets fan (Eric) waiting for the moment of truth:

7. When I was in high school the Steelers played in a Superbowl against Dallas. I went to a Superbowl party because there was free beer and ended up rooting for Dallas just to piss off my classmates, frat boy types that I hated. I think they almost killed me that night. It was the first time I saw a guy almost cry.

8. The Steelers won that game with a field goal and lost the AFC Championship to the New England Patriots, a team I have grown to hate even though my dad's family is from the Boston area. Not like they cared about football but still.

9. Superbowl wins in 2005 and 2008.

10. 2 ridiculous losses to the Oakland Raiders come to mind.

The Second Life
Edwin Morgan

But does every man feel like this at forty -
I mean it's like Thomas Wolfe's New York, his
heady light, the stunning plunging canyons, beauty -
pale stars winking hazy downtown quitting-time,
and the winter moon flooding the skyscrapers, northern -
an aspiring place, glory of the bridges, foghorns
are enormous messages, a looming mastery
that lays its hand on the young man's bowels
until he feels in that air, that rising spirit
all things are possible, he rises with it
until he feels that he can never die -
Can it be like this, and is this what it means
in Glasgow now, writing as the aircraft roar
over building sites, in this warm west light
by the daffodil banks that were never so crowded and lavish -
green May, and the slow great blocks rising
under yellow tower cranes, concrete and glass and steel
out of a dour rubble it was and barefoot children gone -
Is it only the slow stirring, a city's renewed life
that stirs me, could it stir me so deeply
as May, but could May have stirred
what I feel of desire and strength
like an arm saluting a sun?

All January, all February the skaters
enjoyed Bingham's pond, the crisp cold evenings,
they swung and flashed among car headlights,
the drivers parked round the unlit pond
to watch them, and give them light, what laughter
and pleasure rose in the rare lulls
of the yards-away stream of wheels along Great Western Road!
The ice broke up, but the boats came out.
The painted boats are ready for pleasure.
The long light needs no headlamps.

Black oar cuts a glitter: it is heaven on earth.

Is it true that we come alive
not once, but many times?
We are drawn back to the image
of the seed in darkness, or the greying skin
of the snake that hides a shining one -
it will push that used-up matter off
and even the film of the eye is sloughed -
That the world may be the same, and we are not
and so the world is not the same,
the second eye is making again
this place, these waters and these towers,
they are rising again
as the eye stands up to the sun,
as the eye salutes the sun.

Many things are unspoken
in the life of a man, and with a place

there is an unspoken love also
in undercurrents, drifting, waiting its time.
A great place and its people are not renewed lightly.
The caked layers of grime
grow warm, like homely coats.
But yet they will be dislodged
and men will still be warm.
The old coats are discarded.
The old ice is loosed.
The old seeds are awake.

Slip out of darkness, it is time.

Second Lives
David Kinloch

Leaves turn sere and there are bings
from networks stretching in through the window:
you could tiptoe now among the stubby thumbs of the city.

You'd like to go but a man –a boy?–
has reached the chimney breast
crawling along the chip pipe, a green can
slung round his neck; with one hand
he reaches for it and sprays 'VOMIT',
spelled with an 'e', on the Victorian
brickwork. I tip my tip and tilt,
let in late sun, exchange a nod.

Does every man or woman feel like this at 51?
It's not like Edwin Morgan's Glasgow but is –
puddles still have hackles, choughs,
working in twos for safety,
have replaced the lamp-lit starlings.
Even the slip roads are extensions.
The strawberry verandah is flash
frozen and exhibited somewhere converted.
The smoke from a cigarette would have sex
if it were presented on a plate but right now
just wants to lie down.

This evening, I'll play O'Hara, and stroll
into 'Revolver', listen to ambient Gaga,
before making for the Red Roof Flats
where my mirror academic – he also likes to slum it –
will feed me paella, regale us with the blood
that dripped through his ceiling
after the upstairs fight. From the balcony
we look down towards the long gone shipyards.

Suddenly we're distracted: a police
helicopter pinpoints a tiny looter
with a doll making for a playpark.
Loudspeakers reverberate among
the towerblocks; the machine
swoops down from its computer game.
I go home to bed.

There, I dream of Stephen, blond,
6ft 2, 42, 32, who lives on Estragon,
latterly named the second library planet
of his Universe, and vow to buck up:
he has just downloaded my poem
to his data helmet and is comparing
it to Edwin Morgan's called
'The Second Life'. He's slightly
crestfallen and in my dream,
so am I.

Tomorrow there will be asian boys
in souped up Mercedes at the corner
with their attractive bangled wrists.

Ah, there is still so much to see
from my rear window. And the Tesco's
lad –Lancelot, yes really– will call.
On telly an aftermath is being concerted.

The question is how to stick it
together, so the rush is felt not fake.
The sweep, the push, the pull.
the salute, the mastery, the bowels,
the missing letters…ach….
Here is that snake in the gut,
biting its own tail even as it shauchles
off the trauchle of 51 lives.
We constantly flake
and remain. It is time

not to bury or to praise you;
simply to let your ash float slightly
up and then into the stream with you
and let Mark scratch his graffiti
on the stone dyke wall:
'EM was here and is'

Seconds

'Second Lives' riffs on one of Edwin Morgan's most famous poems 'The Second Life'. Morgan (1920-2010) was one of a handful of major 20th century Scottish poets and in his old age became first Glasgow's then Scotland's national 'makar' or laureate. This poem gave its title to his important 1968 collection which also contains many other celebrated poems such as 'The Death of Marilyn Monroe', concrete poems like 'Message Clear' and 'Canedolia' as well as the best of his short love lyrics and at least two of the distinctive science fiction poems. The collection's diversity and sheer verve suggests that the ecstatic hopefulness expressed by 'The Second Life' was certainly not without foundation if set in the context of Morgan's own development as a poet. But the sense of personal renewal transmitted by this poem seeks to root itself also in the material changes that were beginning to transform the cityscape of Glasgow in the 1960s. This decade saw the clearance of notorious tenement slums and their replacement by tower blocks. In their turn many of these new buildings would become a problematic solution to economic and social deprivation but in his 1968 poem Morgan gives them a heroic character appropriate to 'an aspiring place' and links them to New York's skyscrapers. Morgan was an early aficionado of the Beat Generation and the up-beat, rangy, excited, slightly helter-skelter on-rush of the verse syntax nods implicitly in their direction. This is complemented, however, by a kind of rhetorical flourish situated in the dependence on types of repetition and in the echo of HughMacDiarmid's late style as the poem presents us with the image of the self renewing snake. Indeed just as the poem threads together all the myriad instances of life that give the poet hope in the future so, stylistically, it weaves an unusual hybrid of tones and voices.

This is a city poem but, as in so many other Morgan city poems, the sounds of nature are rarely excluded and come to mingle with the traffic. The skaters of Bingham's pond are spied from a city balcony -the poet's own- not mentioned in this poem but the site of one of his most moving love poems placed later in the same collection. This love is of the 'unspoken' variety Morgan had to suppress so painfully until he came out as a gay man in 1990 at the age of seventy. And yet, in this poem where nothing, apparently, can be negative, it takes on the force of a natural 'undercurrent...waiting its time'.

Read in 2011 in a Glasgow that is the same in many ways yet also profoundly different, 'The Second Life' ignites both uplift and dyspepsia. My poem rifles Morgan's most celebrated stanzas for their images, facets, tones, aiming at a different confection and stands in admiration before the sheer grandeur of his verse.

David Kinloch | *Glasgow*

I live on a street called 'Prospecthill Road' and I can see
all of the city spread out beneath me from the windows of
my flat. In that sense I live with 'Glasgow' constantly in
view; ideas about and generated by the city seem to hover
on the horizon whenever I walk into my sitting room and
look out the window. Does that mean that everything I
write is infused with an implicit 'Weegieness' whether the
city is the actual topic or not? My writing table –which is
also my dinner table and general rubbish dump in times
of fraughtness- faces the view. I can't get away from it.
But often I'm sceptical: it's just a place I work –a lot!
There are days when the gothic spires of Glasgow University away to the West or the Cathedral away to the East
are punctuation to passages of boredom I could well do
without. And then a cirrus cloud will settle high above the
low rise of the distant Campsie Hills and something like
a thought will occur. I was born somewhere in this view
and I live there, mostly. I sure as hell don't intend to die
in it though!

Biographies

Jane Bernstein is the author of five books, among them the memoirs Bereft - *A Sister's Story*, and *Rachel in the World*. Her awards include two National Endowment Fellowships, two Pennsylvania Council on the Art Fellowships, and a 2004 Fulbright Fellowship spent in Israel, where she taught at Bar-Ilan University's Creative Writing Program. Her essays have been published in such places as the New York Times Magazine, Ms., Prairie Schooner, Poets & Writers, Self, and Creative Nonfiction, and her screenwork includes the screenplay for the Warner Brothers movie Seven Minutes in Heaven. Jane, a member of the Creative Writing at Carnegie Mellon University, is working on a new novel, *The Face Tells the Secret*.

Alistair Braidwood was born in the English city of Bradford but was smuggled north of the border six months later. Since then he has lived and breathed in Glasgow. In 2011 he received his PhD in Scottish Literature from the University of Glasgow and is a writer, reviewer, commentator and critic on Scottish culture. He runs the website Scots Whay Hae! and hosts the accompanying podcast. He also writes Indelible Ink, a monthly column on modern Scottish Literature for the website Dear Scotland and has published on Scottish film, Robert Burns, contemporary Scottish literature and the philosophy of literature. He is an Editor at Cargo Publishing.

Charlee Brodsky, a fine art documentary photographer and a professor of photography at Carnegie Mellon University, describes her work as dealing with social issues and beauty. She is delighted to be *Pittsburgh's Artist of the Year* - 2012, an award given annually by the

Pittsburgh Center for the Arts. Brodsky often works with writers—both dead and alive. In her recent work, she and her dog Max collaborate with masters such as Shakespeare, Beckett, and Dostoyevsky to produce hand-made books. Prior to this her books include *From Mall Town to Mill Town*, with Jim Daniels and Jane McCafferty; *I Thought I Could Fly… Portraits of Anguish, Compulsion*, and *Despair; Street*, with Jim Daniels; *Knowing Stephanie*, with Stephanie Byram and Jennifer Matesa. Brodsky walks Pittsburgh streets everyday with her two Westies, Max and Sam. To learn more about Charlee Brodsky, please visit her site: www.charleebrodsky.com.

Gordon Burniston is a 28 year old photographer from Glasgow, Scotland. www.burniston.com

Peter Mackie Burns is a multi award- winning Director whose work includes *Milk*, which won numerous awards around the world including the Golden Bear for Best Short Film at the Berlin Film Festival in 2005. He then wrote and directed the short film *Run* for the BBC before directing a Coming Up for Channel 4 called *The Spastic King* from a script by Jack Thorne. Over the past two years he has been directing a non- fiction feature entitled *Come Closer* and has recently completed another short film, *Stronger*, based on the work of August Strindberg. Peter is represented by Sean Gascoine at United Agents.

Andrew Mellon Professor Douglas Cooper has taught drawing in Carnegie Mellon's School of Architecture since 1976. For the last 15 years he has focused on large panoramic murals (up to 200 feet-long and 15 feet-high) in various cities: world-wide. In many of these projects he has worked collaboratively with other artists, with his own students, and with the local populace to incorporate the life stories of a city into the works: often with drawings by residents and with stories in their own languages. These murals present a highly personal record of the urban life of each city. Cities where he has completed murals are: Frankfurt (Kleinemarkthalle); Doha, Qatar; New York (John's Pizzeria); Philadelphia (County Courthouse); Pittsburgh (CMU: University Center) (Senator John Heinz History Center); Rome (University of Rome "la Sapienza); San Francisco (UCSF: Medical Sciences Building); Seattle (King County Courthouse). His most recent work is directed at using his drawings as a background setting for animated films. To date, working with recent CMU graduate Ryan Woodring, two films have been completed: *Pinburgh* 2010 and *Hill Dancers*, the latter also with CMU faculty Jane Bernstein and Thomas Douglas.

Sharon Dilworth is the author of two collections of short stories, *The Long White* and *Women Drinking Benedictine*. Last year she published the novel *Year of the Ginkgo*, which is about a woman who has an unrequited crush on her Scottish neighbor, and later develops an obsession with all things Scottish, so Sharon is particularly happy to be included this anthology. An associate professor of English at Carnegie Mellon University, she is also the fiction editor at Autumn House Press in Pittsburgh.

Rodge Glass is the author of the novels *No Fireworks* (Faber, 2005) and *Hope for Newborns* (Faber, 2008), as well as *Alasdair Gray: A Secretary's Biography* (Bloomsbury, 2008), which received a Somerset Maugham Award in 2009. He was co-author of the graphic novel *Dougie's War: A Soldier's Story* (Freight, 2010), which was nominated for several awards. His new novel, *Bring Me the Head of Ryan Giggs*, was published in April 2012. He is currently a Lecturer at Strathclyde University, also Associate Editor at Cargo Publishing where he has worked on books such as *The Year of Open Doors* and Allan Wilson's *Wasted in Love*. In September 2012 he takes up a post as Senior Lecturer in Creative Writing at Edge Hill University.

Charlotte Glynn was born in New York and spent her formative years in Pittsburgh PA. In 2009 she finished her first feature film, *Rachel is*, a documentary about her sister who is developmentally disabled. *Rachel is*, distributed by Seventh Art Releasing, has screened internationally, including the True/False Film Festival and won best documentary at the Thin Line Documentary Film Festival and Athens International Film Festival. Charlotte was named one of the 10 Filmmakers to Watch in 2010 by *The Independent*. She has also received a Pennsylvania Council for the Arts Fellowship in Media Arts, two Heinz Endowment, and residencies with the Lower Manhattan Cultural Council and the Virginia Center for the Creative Arts among others. She lives in Brooklyn with her dog Becky and is working on the next two installments of the Pittsburgh Trilogy (football and gymnastics) and pursuing her MFA in Film at Columbia University School of the Arts.

Lee Gutkind, recognized by Vanity Fair as "the Godfather behind creative nonfiction," is author and editor of more than 20 books and founder and editor of Creative Nonfiction, the first and largest literary magazine to publish nonfiction exclusively. He is the Distinguished Writer-in-Residence in the Consortium for Science, Policy & Outcomes at Arizona State University and a professor in the Hugh Downs School of Human Communication. Gutkind has lectured to audiences around the world—from China to the Czech Republic, from Australia to Africa to Egypt. He has appeared on many national television shows including Good Morning America and The Daily Show (Comedy Central) with Jon Stewart. Gutkind is Professor Emeritus at the University of Pittsburgh where he taught before assuming his current position in Arizona. At Pitt, he founded the University of Pittsburgh Writers Conference, chaired the Student Publications Board and helped launch the creative writing MFA program. He is the recipient of grants and awards from many different organizations, including the National Endowment for the Arts to the National Science Foundation. A prolific author, his most recent books include *An Immense New Power to Heal: The Promise of Personalized Medicine, You Can't Make This Stuff Up! True Stories Well Told* and an edited anthology, *At the End of Life: True Stories About How We Die*. For more information see: www.leegutkind. com, www.creativenonfiction.org

Yona Harvey is a literary artist residing in Pittsburgh, Pennsylvania, USA. She is the author of the poetry collection, *Hemming the Water* (Four Way Books: New York, 2013), and directs the Creative Writing Program at Carnegie Mellon University.

Terrance Hayes was born in Columbia, South Carolina in 1971. He received a B.A. from Coker College in Hartsville, South Carolina, and an M.F.A. from the University of Pittsburgh writing program. He is the author of *Lighthead* (Penguin, 2010), which won the National Book Award for Poetry; *Wind in a Box* (2006); *Hip Logic* (2002), which won the 2001 National Poetry Series and was a finalist for the Los Angeles Times Book Award; and *Muscular Music* (1999), winner of the Kate Tufts Discovery Award.

Lori Jakiela is the author of a memoir, *Miss New York Has Everything* (Hatchette, 2006), and a poetry collection – *Spot the Terrorist!* (Turning Point, 2012). Her essays and poems have been published in The New York Times, The Washington Post, The Chicago Tribune, The Pittsburgh Post-Gazette, Creative Nonfiction, 5 AM, Tears in the Fence (U.K.) and elsewhere. Her second memoir, *The Bridge to Take When Things Get Serious*, is forthcoming from C&R Press in 2013. She teaches in the writing programs at The University of

Pittsburgh-Greensburg and Chatham University. She lives in her hometown – Trafford, Pennsylvania – with her writer/husband Dave Newman and their two children. For more, visit: www.lorijakielawritesbooks.com

Doug Johnstone is a writer, journalist and musician based in Edinburgh. His most recent novel, *Hit & Run*, was published by Faber and Faber in March 2012. His previous novels are *Smokeheads* (2011), *The Ossians* (2008) and *Tombstoning* (2006). His work has received praise from the likes of Irvine Welsh and Ian Rankin. Between 2010 and 2012 Doug was Writer in Residence at the University of Strathclyde. He's had short stories published in various collections and magazines, and since 1999 has worked as a freelance arts journalist, currently writing for *The Independent on Sunday*, *Scotland on Sunday*, *The Scotsman*, *The Herald* and *The Big Issue* magazine amongst others. Doug is also a singer, musician and songwriter in several bands, including Northern Alliance, part of the Fence Collective. Northern Alliance have released four albums to critical acclaim, as well as recording an album as a fictional band called The Ossians. Doug released his debut solo EP, *Keep it Afloat*, in 2011. For more please visit: dougjohnstone.wordpress.com and dougjohnstone.bandcamp.com

Kapka Kassabova grew up in Bulgaria and her family emigrated to New Zealand after the fall of the Berlin Wall. She is the author of two poetry collections, *Someone Else's Life* and *Geography for the Lost* (Bloodaxe), and her childhood memoir of Communist Bulgaria, *Street Without a Name* (Portobello 2008), was short-listed for the Prix du livre européen and the Dolmann Travel Club Book Award. *Villa Pacifica*, her mystery novel, came out in 2011 (Alma). Her new memoir *Twelve Minutes of Love* is a story of Argentine tango and obsession, and has been short-listed for the 2012 Scottish Book

Awards. Kapka's books have sold rights into Spanish, Russian, Bulgarian, Czech, Swedish, Hebrew and Japanese. She is a regular contributor for The Guardian and Granta magazine. She lives in Edinburgh and the Scottish Highlands, and is this year's Shakespeare Birthplace Writer in Residence in Stratford-upon-Avon.

Jackie Kay was born in Edinburgh, Scotland and brought up in Glasgow. Her first collection of poetry, *The Adoption Papers*, was published in 1991. Her first novel, *Trumpet*, published in 1998, was awarded the Guardian fiction prize and was shortlisted for the International Impac Dublin literary award. Other books include the short story collections of, *Why Don't You Stop Talking* (2002) and *Wish I Was Here* (2006), a novel for children, *Strawgirl* (2002) a novella, *Sonata* (2006) and autobiography, *Red Dust Road* (2010). 2011's poetry collection *Fiere* was shortlisted for the Costa Book Awards and her latest book is *Reality, Reality*; a collection of short stories. In 2006, she was awarded an MBE for services to literature and she is currently the Professor for Creative Writing at Newcastle University.

David Kinloch was born and brought up in Glasgow, Scotland. He is a graduate of the Universities of Glasgow and Oxford and was for many years a teacher of French. He currently teaches Creative Writing and Scottish literature at the University of Strathclyde, Glasgow where he is Reader in Poetry. A winner of the Robert Louis Stevenson Memorial Award, he is the author of five collections of poetry including *Un Tour d'Ecosse* (2001), *In My Father's House* (2005) and *Finger of a Frenchman* (2011), all from Carcanet. In the 1980s he co-founded and co-edited the influential poetry magazine, *Verse*. More recently he helped establish the first ever Scottish Writers' Centre and is a founder and organiser of the Edwin Morgan International Poetry Competition. His personal website is at www.davidkinloch.co.uk

Hilary Masters grew up in Kansas City, Missouri and attended public schools there. He enlisted in the Navy at the end of World War II and then graduated from Brown University. He has published novels, short stories and personal essays and now lives in Pittsburgh, PA.

Jane McCafferty is author of four books of fiction, most recently the novel *First You Try Everything* (HarperCollins 2012.) She is winner of an NEA, the Drue Heinz prize for fiction, two Pushcart prizes, and The Great Lake New Writers Award. Her stories and poems and essays have appeared in a variety of journals. She teaches at Carnegie Mellon in Pittsburgh.

Mitch Miller is an illustrator and writer who lives in Glasgow. In 2001 he co-founded The Drouth magazine and has published books, essays and articles on subjects such as Scottish Politics, the politics of Scottish writers, Travelling Showpeople, Gypsies and other travellers, home-made experimental cinema and Glasgow's visual arts scene. Past projects include the web-documentary Boswell in Space (www.boswellinspace.org) and a period as resident artist at the Red Road Flats. He has exhibited his work in museums, tower blocks, Scottish islands, caravans (or trailers as Americans and travellers would have it), temporary exhibition spaces and actual galleries. Mitch is currently pursuing his insane scheme to draw the entirety of Glasgow in dialectogram form as part of a practice-based PhD at the Glasgow School of Art.

Ewan Morrison is the author of some books. He is a cultural commentator and a renaissance man who has run out of money.

Brian O'Neill is the author of *The Paris of Appalachia: Pittsburgh in the Twenty-first Century*, the only book in the history of books that's sold both at the Carnegie Museum of Art and Gus Kalaris's ice-ball stand on the city's North Side. He's been a newspaper columnist in Pittsburgh for almost a quarter-century, but only recently has "Glaswegian" become one of his favorite words to say out loud. He hopes the Scots feel the same about "Pittsburgher."

Will Self is the author of twenty-one books, most of which are fiction in one form or another. He's a regular broadcaster on television and radio, and a prolific contributor to a wide span of publications from the *London Review of Books* to *Playboy* (US), to the *New York Times* to the *Scotsman* (for which he once syndicated a column under the bizarre heading 'The Bloke from the Smoke') and back again. He lives in South London and is currently the Professor of Contemporary Thought at Brunel University.

Gerald Stern was born in Pittsburgh, Pennsylvania in 1925 and was educated at the University of Pittsburgh and Columbia University. He is the author of 15 books of poetry, including, most recently, *Save the Last Dance* (Norton, 2008) and *Everything is Burning* (Norton, 2005), as well as *This Time: New and Selected Poems*, which won the 1998 National Book Award. The paperback of his personal essays titled *What I Can't Bear Losing*, was published in the fall of 2009 by Trinity University Press. He was awarded the 2005 Wallace Stevens Award by the Academy of American Poets and is currently a Chancellor of the Academy of American Poets. He is retired from the University of Iowa Writers' Workshop. *Early Collected: Poems from 1965-1992* was published by W. W.

Norton in the spring of 2010. Stern's *Stealing History*, a kind-of memoir, was published in early 2012 by Trinity University Press. A new book of poems from W. W. Norton, *In Beauty Bright*, will be released in the fall of 2012.

Louise Welsh is the author of five novels including 'The Girl on the Stairs' which will be published by John Murray in August 2012. She has been the recipient of several awards and fellowships, including an honorary fellowship from the University of Iowa's International Writing programme. Louise was writer in residence at the University of Glasgow and Glasgow School of Art 2010-2012. Louise has also written plays, short stories, articles, sound scapes and libretti for opera. 'Ghost Patrol', a new opera with music by Stuart McRae, libretto by Louise Welsh, will be produced by Scottish Opera at 2012's Edinburgh International Festival. She lives in Glasgow with the author Zoe Strachan. www.louisewelsh.com

Allan Wilson is from Glasgow. His short story collection *Wasted in Love* was published by Cargo in October 2011 and has been short-listed for The Scottish Book of the Year Award 2012. He is currently working on his first novel, *Meat*.

Richard Wilson was born in Glasgow, educated in Glasgow, married in Glasgow and is bringing up his two children in Glasgow. He is a sportswriter with *The Herald* and *Sunday Herald* newspapers and author of *Inside The Divide*, a book about the Old Firm rivalry between Rangers and Celtic. His earlier career was spent at *The Sunday Times Scotland*, where he was deputy sports editor then sportswriter. In 2002 he won the Jim Rodger Memorial Award for best young sports writer. In 2003 at the Scottish Press Awards, he was named Sports Writer of the Year, and he has regularly been nominated in the Sports Feature Writer of the Year category.

Credits

This book was only possible because of the generosity of a number of contributors in allowing us to reproduce, quote from, or use extracts from their work. Detailed below are those whom we are indebted to:

"The Organ Grinder" by Eduard Bersudsky is reproduced here courtesy of The Sharmanka Gallery.

Excerpt from "Between Shadow and Light" by Douglas Cooper is from Steel Shadows. Murals and Drawings of Pittsburgh by Douglas Cooper. © 2000. Reprinted by permission of the University of Pittsburgh Press.

"Working the Red Eye, From Pittsburgh to Vegas," "No Amount of Money Can Get You a Better Coke Than the One the Bum on the Corner is Drinking," "Mill Hunk," and "Machine," are reprinted by permission of Lori Jakiela.

Jackie Kay's poem "The Shoes of Dead Comrades" was first published in her collection Off Colour, published by Bloodaxe Books, 1999.

Excerpt from "Passing Through Pittsburgh" by Hilary Masters originally appeared in Creative Nonfiction: Issue 15. Reprinted by permission of the Creative Nonfiction Foundation.

Edwin Morgan's poem 'The Second Life' was originally published in The Second Life, Edinburgh
University Press, 1968. It is reprinted here courtesy of The Estate of Edwin Morgan, also with thanks to Michael Schmidt and to Carcanet Press.

Will Self's piece "Night Walk" was an essay first written for broadcast on BBC Radio 3.

"The Train Station," from Stealing History by Gerald Stern. © 2012. Reprinted by permission of Trinity University Press.

We would also like to thank Denise Noone for her stunning photography which we used to make the book cover.